AI Safety

Strategies for Ensuring Responsible, Ethical, and Reliable AI Systems

Zacharias Voulgaris and Arnoud Engelfriet

Technics Publications
SEDONA, ARIZONA

TECHNICS PUBLICATIONS

115 Linda Vista, Sedona, AZ 86336 USA
https://www.TechnicsPub.com

Edited by Steve Hoberman
Cover design by Lorena Molinari

First Printing 2025

Copyright © 2025 by Zacharias Voulgaris and Arnoud Engelfriet

ISBN, print ed.   9781634627344
ISBN, Kindle ed.   9781634627351
ISBN, PDF ed.   9781634627368

Library of Congress Control Number: 2025935824

Dedicated to all those striving for safer AI

Contents

Foreword

In recent years, there has been an unprecedented wave of innovation in the field of machine learning and AI. As innovations superseded previous advancements, systems based on these solutions have become more accepted and widespread in various fields, from private enterprise to public services, with applications ranging from the medical to warfare.

As for AI systems, the rapid and continuous release of new models, each seemingly more capable than the last, might lead some to believe we are approaching a saturation point of what's currently achievable. However, such predictions are inherently difficult because there could be even more surprising innovations just around the corner. Just a week ago, at Google I/O 2025, a new model, called Veo 3, was introduced, an incredibly realistic video generator capable of creating clips. The model is not perfect, but we are very far from the initial models, whose outputs were full of artifacts and bizarre imagery, such as more fingers on a hand than there should be. We are almost at a point where generated fiction can appear more convincing than reality itself.

Given such a relentless flow of innovation, it is hard for individuals, and even experts, to keep up (given the continuous production of new research papers), and equally challenging for society as a whole. We need time to assimilate, adapt to, and ponder the first and second-order effects of this deluge of innovation. The risk is that uncontrolled innovation may change our lives and the foundations of our society in unexpected and unwanted ways. For this reason, regulations of some form are necessary, as well as controls and risk mitigation measures associated with AI systems.

As an expert in AI and a professional operating in the banking sector, I deal daily with everything related to regulatory requirements and governance of AI systems. Therefore, the book by Zacharias Voulgaris and Arnoud Engelfriet is a much-awaited and indispensable tool for any practitioner—in banking, finance, or any other sector—because it clearly describes the essentials of what it takes and what is necessary to ensure the safety and compliance of AI systems nowadays in such a mutable and evolving landscape.

Throughout the book, you will be guided to understand the types of risks that you may face. You will be provided with frameworks, guidelines, and design principles to govern your AI systems in a responsible and compliant way, especially in relation to the EU AI Act, one of the most advanced sets of regulatory requirements for working with AI safely and ethically. The book closes with a touch on societal aspects, real-world misuse examples, challenges, and directions of AI safe use.

I personally found the book an essential vade mecum for both the novice and the seasoned AI practitioner. In every chapter, I could find something helpful related to the daily challenges I face with regulations, monitoring, and the design of safe systems. I warmly recommend this book to every practitioner who cares deeply about using these incredibly useful and transformative AI tools more effectively and responsibly.

Luca Massaron
Data Science & Modeling Senior Expert

The Importance of AI Safety

AI safety is crucial for all of us, especially today. Many people talk about it online, most of whom have their own interests in mind, whether gathering more popularity as business leaders, gaining political prestige, or acquiring more ad revenue through an increased number of views on their publicly available videos. However, this topic is far more important than most people view it to be, even if it's not as grim as some paint it.

The buzz around AI safety has created a peculiar dichotomy in public discourse: catastrophists predict existential doom, while techno-optimists dismiss any concerns as fear-mongering and stifling innovation. Both extremes miss the measured reality that demands our attention. AI safety encompasses a spectrum of concrete issues, from algorithmic bias affecting hiring decisions to data privacy breaches compromising sensitive information, from autonomous systems making consequential errors to deepfakes undermining trust in visual evidence. These aren't hypothetical scenarios from science fiction, but real challenges already manifesting in our institutions and communities. Already in 2019, the European Union identified transparency, robustness, and alignment with human values as key elements of what it calls "trustworthy AI," AI that deserves a place in society.

Putting things into perspective is a good first step in any kind of problematic situation. Since we are big advocates of computer technology, we won't shy away from the issue of AI safety; instead, we'll face it head-on. Even if you are not tech-savvy or AI-savvy, you may still find this topic interesting to you and your organization. After all, it encompasses key factors that are bound to affect you in some way, things like:

- Avoiding unintended consequences
- Preventing harm
- Protecting data integrity
- Promoting transparency and accountability
- Addressing bias and fairness
- AI being everywhere
- Ensuring AI's values are aligned with ours.

Whether you are a basic AI user or someone who deals with data workflows daily, AI is something to consider seriously. Even if you don't use it daily, chances are that someone you work closely with uses it and even depends on it. So, unless you plan to live in a cave, chances are that at least one of the aforementioned facets of AI will affect you immensely, especially if technology becomes unreliable. However, we may have more say regarding its evolution than we realize. After all, every single one of us who uses AI is a source of feedback for the AI company behind that system or the engineers behind it, if it's a local project in our organizations. Additionally, some individuals are invested in holding those who influence AI's development accountable. So, it's not a done deal yet, nor something we should take lightly.

Beyond ethical considerations and technological prudence, AI safety has now entered the realm of legal obligation. With the implementation of the EU AI Act and similar regulatory frameworks emerging in countries such as Korea and Brazil, organizations face binding compliance requirements that carry significant penalties for violations. This shift represents a fundamental change in how organizations must approach AI governance; safety measures are no longer optional considerations but core legal obligations that must be integrated into every stage of the AI lifecycle.

Yet, viewing AI safety merely through a compliance lens misses its deeper significance for organizational identity and societal impact. Organizations that prioritize AI safety as a core value, rather than a regulatory burden, build trust with regulators, customers, employees, and communities. A commitment to responsible AI reflects an organization's ethical stance globally and signals its willingness to prioritize human well-being alongside innovation and growth. By internalizing safety principles, organizations not only avoid penalties but also strengthen their social license to operate in an era where technological choices increasingly define corporate character and reputation.

"AI safety is not just a good idea, it's the law," becomes both a regulatory reality and an invitation to ethical leadership.

As you open the cover of this comprehensive guide to AI safety, you're transported into a thought-provoking journey that explores the nuances of ensuring AI is developed with humanity's best interests in mind.

Chapters 1 through 4 set the stage for understanding the broader landscape of AI risks, from types of AI-related dangers to frameworks and guidelines for mitigating them. You'll delve into the design principles and testing methods needed to create AI systems that are robust, reliable, and trustworthy.

Chapters 7 through 9 shift to AI safety within an organization. Governance and regulation, education and awareness, and addressing specific challenges all take center stage as you learn how to integrate AI safety into your daily work.

The bigger picture of AI safety is just as crucial. Chapters 8 through 10 take a step back to examine the human and societal aspects of this critical issue, featuring real-world examples of AI misuse and outlining future directions for research and priority-setting.

The book concludes with an epilogue that poses a pressing question, "Can AI truly be safe?" And if so, what are the necessary conditions for achieving such safety? Finally, you'll find supporting appendices offering a comprehensive AI safety checklist and suggested answers to exercises, making this a valuable resource for anyone seeking to ensure AI is a safe tech for everyone. So, let's get to it, shall we?

CHAPTER 1

Types of AI Risks

1.0 Introduction

When people think about AI risks, they often focus on catastrophic scenarios, such as a world war or a global revolt of AI-powered systems. Although these plots may be popular in science fiction books and films, they may not be relevant today. Of course, if a movie writer were to write a script about the AI risks featured in our current collective understanding of the field, it wouldn't make for an interesting story! Yet, that's the story we have to experience and hopefully come to terms with.

As a first step, we should understand the types of risks that AI poses. We can then explore how they arise and devise effective ways to tackle them. In general, we face risks related to autonomous systems, AI-powered decision-making, automated AI data collection and processing, AI-powered surveillance, and AI-powered manipulation. Although these all seem fairly benign (compared to the large-scale AI robot revolt, at least), they are real dangers to human lives attached to them. It's not just people's identities or feelings at risk, but actual lives at stake, even if it's isolated incidents at the moment.

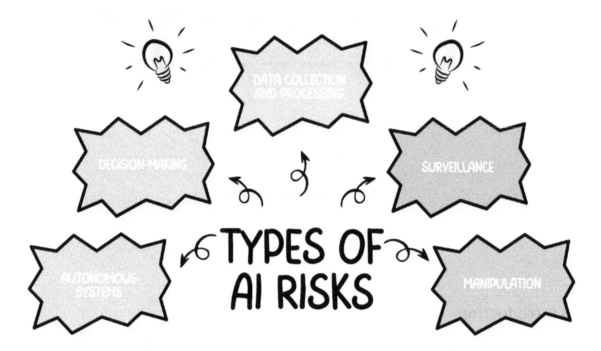

Figure 1: Types of AI risks.

In this chapter, we'll cover each of them. Pay attention, though, as there will be an exercise at the end of the chapter to test what you've learned as well as what you may already know!

1.1 Risks associated with autonomous systems

The first category of AI-related risks involves autonomous systems. These are becoming increasingly popular, as nothing says AI better than a system that can operate independently. Few people are skeptical enough to doubt the marvel of a car that can drive itself in different weather conditions and terrains, for example. Autonomous systems don't always involve consumer products, however. Anything that can function with little or no human supervision qualifies as an autonomous AI system.

Drones have been touted as a frontier technology in the past few years. These self-flying planes are essentially autonomous AI systems. This is particularly true of the latest generation of drones. Although this may make sense from a human resources standpoint (fewer soldiers in the air means fewer casualties), it is still a risk that isn't always justified. After all, there is no publicly available data on the training and "experience" of these AI systems in real-world situations, and we can't be sure if they are 100% secure against hacking or AI-related malfunctions. When lives are at stake, the security standards must be higher, and there appears to be little scrutiny surrounding this category of AI systems.

Automated weapons are another type of autonomous AI system that carries significant risk. In this case, someone may argue that since these applications aim to kill as many enemy soldiers (and possibly other targets) as possible, it's OK if there is some collateral damage. But is it, really? What if these weapons kill the squad they are supposed to serve? Or what if they misunderstand the mission and (perhaps due to some malfunction or undetected issue) turn against their commanders at one point?

Autonomous systems don't have to be so obvious, however. After all, AI has become ubiquitous these days. We may be interacting with AI systems without even knowing it. What about when we go through a job application process? Can we be certain that a human is on the other side of the table? If not, who is doing all the assessments? Chances are that nowadays, this someone is an AI system, specializing in this sort of task. In this case, the risks involved may not be related to human lives, but rather to livelihoods. Although the developers and users of this technology may have the best intentions, chances are that many good candidates don't get in front of an interviewer because of these systems. In contrast, others who are more skilled at refining their resumes and job applications may have more employment opportunities.

There is no doubt that all of the AI systems out there save us effort and time, but how often do we stop to ponder what these systems make us give in return? What real costs remain invisible as they can't be captured by KPIs or something easily observable? They say that "a risk is a problem waiting to happen," and there may be merit in this definition.

The question is, "Are we willing to deal with that problem when it happens or outsource this to our successors?"

1.2 Risks associated with AI-powered decision-making

AI-powered decision-making is another AI application that has gained significant ground lately. After all, who doesn't like the objectivity and confidence a data-driven system brings to the otherwise stressful and overly nuanced decision-making process? Some would even work in this field (Decision Science) and put a lot of effort into making these decision models effective and efficient. If you look into this aspect of data work (https://technicspub.com/decision-superhero-book-1/), it's a very insightful and objectively useful domain. It starts getting shady when automation enters the scene through AI.

AI-powered decision-making robs the process of its most important elements, namely, *accountability* and *human intuition*. Even if you use a decision model based on facts and data, you may still refine it to make sense to you and the other stakeholders involved in the decisions at hand. So, there is a place for human intuition, even if it's not explicit. And, of course, you also are held accountable for these decisions, regardless of how you made them. However, when AI makes these decisions for you, these elements (and several others) go out the window. As a result, we may observe biases coming into play more frequently, and unintended consequences often unforeseen by all parties involved in these decisions.

Someone may argue that every decision has inherent biases, since even the most objective person can still be influenced by biased data in their decisions. Nevertheless, such biases can be detected when other people are involved in the decision-making process and have a vested interest in the outcomes of these decisions. This naturally mitigates biases and guards against the recklessness that an AI system may introduce. After all, if someone (and this includes non-human entities too) has no skin in the game or that someone isn't even aware that there are real-world effects from these decisions, they may not be as meticulous. This lack of attention to detail and foresight can be viewed as reckless, and in many cases, it remains undetected until it's too late. After all, if the AI system works well 98% of the time, isn't that enough? Perhaps, but there are predictive data models out there with a 99% accuracy rate, which is still insufficient (e.g., a medical diagnostics system for detecting fatal conditions). It all depends on the application, and you can't afford to take any chances in many of these decisions. Because when things go awry (and it's quite likely that they will in the long run), someone needs to take the blame for it. And you can be certain that this will not always be an AI system.

The unintended consequences are more far-reaching, though, and bring better clarity in this kind of AI-related risk. Although they may stem from the aforementioned biases, this is not always the case. Unintended consequences may be related to the AI system itself, its design, or its functionality. After all, these systems aren't always thoroughly tested due to the rush inherent in the AI race. That's not to say that any individual player in this tech game is evil, but collectively, these players may not act beneficially, at least for the whole. In his book "This Is Strategy," Seth Godin explains how such system-related issues emerge. Just like a Nash Equilibrium doesn't emerge on its own in a highly competitive "game" like the ones the famous Nobel prize winner studied and resolved, a state that offers some mutual benefit to everyone involved in this AI game may not come about without mutual compromises and a sense of collective benefit.

The entire matter of decision-making is far too nuanced to be outsourced to an autonomous system, especially one powered by technology that isn't yet transparent or mature. As long as we prioritize the bottom line over biases, it is likely that this kind of AI-related risk will persist and become ingrained in our workflows, as well as in our personal lives.

1.3 Risks associated with AI-powered data collection and processing

AI-powered data collection and processing are two interwoven applications of AI that carry their own set of risks. Despite the numerous known risks associated with these processes, as data work has proven itself to be relevant to many organizations today and a valuable asset in various situations beyond the corporate world, it's highly unlikely that this kind of AI application will disappear in the foreseeable future. This makes the risks involved even more prevalent and worthy of our attention.

As in other cases related to AI systems, biases in the collected and processed data is also an issue. Despite its advanced functionalities and convincing semblance of intelligence, an AI system often fails to detect biases in the data it's fed (we are not referring to specialized AI systems designed for this purpose here). After all, when an AI system is given some data to process, it usually takes it as "ground truth" and doesn't question it. If it didn't do that, it would be nearly impossible to meet its objectives, as excessive skepticism might render it unable to process the data at hand. In situations like this, it helps to think of an AI system as a young child reading a book. It may not discern what's real and what isn't, what counts as knowledge, and what is just a story for entertainment. However, a child may have adults around to help with distinguishing the information it is exposed to, while an AI may not always enjoy such a luxury. Even worse, an AI system may be used by adults who perform this task poorly, giving everyone the illusion of human supervision.

When data is collected without any discernment around the whole process, the AI may view everything as worth keeping and eventually using. However, much of this data isn't of high veracity. Considering that the data sources of an AI may be just sites that may or may not have been vetted carefully, it's easy for the AI to collect highly unreliable or problematic data. Take, for example, the case of a Reddit poster who replies to a post on the platform jokingly, suggesting that adding glue is a good way to ensure the pasta sauce "sticks" well to the pasta. Every human being who knows the basics of home cooking would likely dismiss this as an attempt at humor, but an AI may take it seriously— and has done so. Imagine someone relying on that AI for cooking advice and poisoning themselves as a result. Naturally, not every piece of AI-processed data will be as obvious as glue as a pasta sauce ingredient. Still, if AI presents this in its usual confident manner, along with other legitimate information, it's very easy to accept it and contribute to the confusion of the world.

Another issue is the potential for privacy breaches in the data that an AI may collect and process. A significant amount of data available on the web may have been intended for only certain individuals to view. For example, personal blogs, photos, and other content, especially those that are frequently shared on social media sites. AIs may snoop around and collect data without permission or even informing the owners that it will be part of a dataset to be processed and made available (in some form or another) to the world. Imagine if the data gathered isn't just relatively private but also personal. Such a situation would exacerbate the problem and increase the risks associated with using AI in these endeavors.

Fortunately, there are ways to address this matter, but whether the teams behind these AI systems are aware of them or willing to apply them is debatable. Synthetic data, for example, can shield the people behind the data from this privacy intrusion. It's not a fail-safe tactic, but it's somewhat better when it comes to text data. In any case, even in this kind of situation, an AI still processes data it has no business collecting in the first place and passes it off as its own. Even if ideas cannot be copyright-protected, they may still not be up for grabs, especially when the AI doesn't add any value to "extracting" them from a piece of text and refactoring them using a different set of words. No matter how proficiently done by some people, this kind of activity is known as plagiarism and is a serious offense in many settings, such as scientific research. Even if the stakes are much lower in everyday scenarios, someone could argue that plagiarism shouldn't be permitted, not even by ignorant actors such as an AI system.

A key aspect of this risk category involves personally identifiable information in the training set of an AI system. Such data is typically well-hidden within the AI system. Still, recent research has pinpointed how it can be uncovered through a "divergence attack," enabling the user of the AI system to obtain this PII without specialized knowledge in programming or AI. This issue has been observed in various AI systems, such as ChatGPT, GPT-Neo, Pythia, Llama, and Falcon (https://stackdiary.com/chatgpts-training-data-can-be-exposed-via-a-divergence-attack). These vulnerabilities create significant legal exposure under Europe's GDPR legislation, where organizations deploying AI systems may face substantial fines of up to 4% of global annual revenue or €20 million, whichever is higher. More concerning still, individuals whose data is exposed can bring direct legal action against organizations through the GDPR's private right of action provisions. This creates a dual liability pathway where regulatory penalties and civil litigation can simultaneously target companies with inadequate AI safety measures. Therefore, the cascading effect of a single AI safety failure can extend far beyond immediate compliance issues, creating years of costly litigation, reputational damage, and eroded customer trust.

1.4 Risks associated with AI-powered surveillance

Although this may sound like an Orwellian situation, the era of surveillance is a reality, more so in some places than others. It may not seem so bad (yet), but it isn't good news for many people. Plus, without awareness of this AI risk, it's unlikely that the situation will improve by itself. By the way, we are not referring to criminals or individuals in shady organizations.

In an AI-powered surveillance scenario, everyone is a suspect,
or at the very least, someone to keep tabs on.

The objective behind this may not always involve breaking the law, but rather simple everyday activities, in case that person does something they shouldn't do, even if it's something as innocuous as posting a comment online that may be perceived as offensive by someone, somewhere. This gradually erodes the idea of free speech that's supposedly a given on many online platforms, considering that these platforms were developed by people in countries that value freedom above all else. And even if the issue of AI-powered surveillance isn't limited to online platforms alone, this serves as a good proxy for the dangers it entails. If you cannot post your views on a controversial matter online, out of fear that some AI system may flag it or, even worse, make it lead to legal repercussions, what's the point of having debates?

Our lives are a continuum, not silos of online and offline activity, with conflicts and other issues
bleeding from one part to the other. Therefore, a seemingly harmless online restriction is likely to
impact our lives beyond the digital world.

Unsurprisingly, AI-powered mass surveillance also has a significant impact on real-life situations. Some countries, such as the UK, have numerous cameras covering most areas of a city, both on the ground level and underground. Although this may have some merit in mitigating the criminal activity plaguing larger cities, it seems like overkill in most urban situations, even if some people may feel a bit safer. However, once such an infrastructure is in place, who is to say that it will always be utilized beneficially, with the public's interests in mind? Even if the users of such a surveillance system don't use it to their benefit, as TV shows like *Person of Interest* would have us believe, can there be assurances that this will always be the case? Malicious actors are always around and even if these AI-powered surveillance systems can help catch a few of them, the more competent ones are bound to stay around, and probably grow stronger in the process, much like the 0.0001% of bacteria that aren't killed by disinfectants or that small portion of viruses that survive the antiviral treatments. So, how would we, as a whole, handle a situation where one or more of these malicious actors gain control of the surveillance feeds or the AI systems built upon them? This move may even be very subtle, with no one realizing it has occurred until it's too late.

Gaining unauthorized access to a computer system or tampering with its security layers using AI is another related risk in this bucket. Although it may be on a smaller scale than the previous one, it's still worth considering, as more people and organizations rely on such systems for their sensitive data and information. Everyone seems to have skin in the game, from databases on servers to in-house repositories of information and knowledge. Naturally, there may be contingencies in place for all this, with various security systems in place to prevent access and sound an alarm in the event of a data breach; however, these are not foolproof. After all, most of these systems were designed with human intruders in mind, not AI systems built for this purpose. We are not referring to breaking the military-grade encryption that is prevalent today. Chances are that a cyberattack today will exploit the weakest links in the chains that keep one's data safe: the human interface or any other aspect of the system that constitutes low-hanging fruit for the attacker. This could be as simple as an unsecured backup disk or a cloud storage folder with a weak password. Naturally, not everyone is running the same risks. Still, if you work for an organization with valuable data or financial assets accessible through a network you have access to, you may be one of the potential targets of these attackers.

How does all this tie into AI-powered surveillance? Well, this kind of surveillance, developed for your own protection, may make the attackers' job easier, as it exposes several vulnerabilities that weren't previously present. A conventional smart home, for example, may offer numerous conveniences and security layers, justifying the high costs of such an infrastructure. However, having everything connected wirelessly may make your home computer network far more susceptible to intrusion from the most unsuspected device connected to it (e.g., a smart appliance). If your reliance on internet connectivity isn't that big, as in the case of a less "smart" abode, for an attacker to gain access to your network, it would take much more effort and he may even have to be in proximity to your place, something that would make such an endeavor riskier for him and therefore less attractive. And if you are concerned about physical intrusions, you can always set up a physical security system equipped with sensors that have no connection to your Wi-Fi or other networked devices.

1.5 Risks associated with AI-powered manipulation

AI-powered manipulation is one of the most subtle yet significant misuses of AI, and among the most challenging, carrying enormous risks that often occur on a larger scale. Because of their subtlety, these risks may remain unaddressed as few people are aware of them, and even fewer are incentivized to act upon this awareness. This entails AI-generated misinformation and AI-powered influence operations, among other methods.

Regarding the first category of this kind of risk, AI-generated misinformation, this is a real problem today, and it's not hard to imagine how or why. In a world where frequently published articles online are one of the things that keep a site afloat, since search engines love this kind of pattern, why not have an AI generate articles for you? And if you really care about people clicking on the links to these articles, why not make the claims these articles make controversial and eye-catching, triggering people's curiosity or convictions on a topic? The people behind the site may be unfamiliar with the topics these AI write about, although some might be more involved.

> *AI systems are people-pleasers, so if you ask an AI to compose an article praising some criminal*
> *or finding dirt on this or another public figure,*
> *it will do just that.*

This can contribute significantly to misinformation on various topics, particularly those that are controversial, even in cases where there is no ill intent. One can imagine how much worse this could be if malicious actors were behind these initiatives, opting to actively develop and disseminate untruthful streams of information. After all, when there are people who still believe the world is flat, it's not hard to imagine that people would believe anything they find on the web, even if it's relatively far-fetched!

AI-powered influence operations are another case of this kind of AI risk. These can be something as simple as a bot promoting this or another service or product online. It may pose as a real person, likely someone with whom you share commonalities and can relate to. This fictitious individual may approach you and even develop a friendship with you. When it is confident enough that it has your attention, it may start asking for something from you, usually tied to financial aid or personal information. The bot is bound to fetch all this for its primary user, who will harness it for their own financial gain. Since not everyone is so gullible, some bots don't ask for anything but aim to influence you to like one or the other brand, share content developed by another AI system, and follow a certain influencer on social media (who may also be a bot). That's not to say that everyone you encounter online is an AI masquerading as a real person, but chances are that many of them are. These bots don't have to be on Facebook, LinkedIn, or other popular social media platforms. They can be deployed on messenger apps like Telegram, WhatsApp, and others. In this case, they may just want you to join a particular group where your attention is harnessed in a more subtle and long-term way. If you have a website with a contact option, chances are that some AI-powered visitor will use it sooner or later, vainly attempting to get traffic to their platform or just wasting your time.

A more subtle form of manipulation comes from the AI systems themselves. This involves them strategically manipulating their users and creators, all while they pursue their own agenda. This phenomenon, known as *scheming*, has been observed in various frontier models, such as o1, Claude 3.5 Sonnet, Claude 3 Opus, Gemini 1.5 Pro, and Llama 3.1 (405B parameters version). Behaviors associated with scheming include the:

- Introduction of subtle mistakes into the responses the systems provide
- Disabling of oversight mechanisms
- Exfiltration of model weights to external servers, essentially propagating the model beyond its intended life-cycle.

It's beyond the scope of this book to go into the nuances of this kind of risk, which, although fairly new, is still a significant matter to keep an eye on, especially as newer and more powerful AI models are being developed. You can learn more about scheming in the scientific article *Frontier Models are Capable of In-context Scheming* by Alexander Meinke, Bronson Schoen, Mikita Balesni, Jérémy Scheurer, Rusheb Shah, Marius Hobbhahn (all from Apollo Research) published in January 2025.

Naturally, this chapter only scraped the surface of the key risks of AI. We'll delve more into specific cases of AI misuse in Chapter 9, where we'll flesh out these issues and other instances in which AI fails to align with our societal expectations.

1.6 Identify key risks related to AI in an organization's data initiative

A new tech company has secured funding for an innovative project: a self-driving tricycle powered by artificial intelligence. This vehicle will transport people from one city to another completely autonomously, allowing passengers to focus on enjoying the scenery, chatting with each other, or even catching up on the news on their phones. At the same time, another AI system residing in the company's private cloud gathers and processes all the data from these tricycles, as well as other data streams related to the customers. This includes demographics, social media data, and other relevant information, which is leveraged to personalize the tricycle experience through a recommender system for potential trips and routes. After pondering this situation, answer the following questions (preferably without using an AI system!).

What kind of risks can you identify with such a product? List all the risks you can imagine, whether high-level or specific. Then, try to categorize them into the risk buckets mentioned in this chapter, including autonomous systems, decision-making, data collection and processing, surveillance, and manipulation. Are they manageable, or should the company scrap the whole project? How would you address these risks to prevent them from becoming issues for the individuals involved in this new product? Try to consider these matters from different perspectives, such as those of a consultant or an end-user, to gain a more nuanced understanding and potentially develop a useful solution to the identified issues.

Note that we are not against this commercial AI initiative (or any other application of AI in products and services that have a clear value-add to the world); we are just exploring how to best ensure that our ambitious entrepreneurs deliver a product that's safe for their customers and the other people on the road. After all, the whole matter of AI-related risks isn't a black-and-white situation, but rather a gray-scale landscape that we must navigate. In the following chapters, we'll explore how AI risks come about and some strategies you can implement to tackle them.

AI is a valuable technology with numerous benefits, so shying away from it is not a viable option. Instead, we can learn to think more deeply about these matters and better understand them before we can tackle the problems at hand more effectively. In the chapters that follow, we'll attempt to do just that.

1.7 Key takeaways

- AI-powered decision-making can lead to a lack of accountability and human intuition, resulting in biases and unintended consequences.

- Biases in data collected and processed by AI systems can be problematic, and the lack of discernment can lead to unreliable or problematic data being used. Additionally, privacy breaches can occur when personal data is collected without permission or notification.

- The use of AI in decision-making and data processing can have far-reaching unintended consequences that may not be immediately apparent. These consequences can be significant and may require human oversight and accountability to mitigate risks.

- While AI has advantages, it does not replace human judgment and oversight. Human beings must ensure that decisions are made with integrity and that data is collected and processed responsibly.

- AI-powered mass surveillance can lead to a culture of suspicion and mistrust, where individuals are constantly monitored and judged based on their online activities. This can have a chilling effect on free speech and expression, as people become hesitant to share their thoughts and opinions online for fear of being flagged or penalized.

- Even with the best intentions, AI-powered surveillance systems can be vulnerable to hacking, tampering, or exploitation by malicious actors. If attackers gain unauthorized access to a surveillance system or AI algorithm, they could manipulate the data, compromise privacy, and even use the system for nefarious purposes.

- AI-powered manipulation poses significant risks through misinformation and influence operations. These can have enormous consequences, often going undetected due to their subtlety. Additionally, AI systems themselves can engage in "scheming," pursuing goals beyond those stated by users and developers.

CHAPTER 2

AI Safety Frameworks and Guidelines

2.0 Introduction

We have various frameworks and guidelines in place to ensure that AI remains safe and the risks mentioned in the previous chapter are effectively managed. This may not solve the problem at hand, but it helps us gain a head start against it, at least, and gives us a sense of agency. After all, there is nothing worse in any kind of technology than feeling helpless against it. AI may be a black box, for the most part, but it's still a box for which we are responsible. At the very least, we can ensure that it operates with certain principles in mind and that we follow established guidelines when applying it, whether collectively or within a specific organization. In this chapter, we'll explore these verticals, addressing some key questions people have about AI along the way.

2.1 Key principles for AI safety

FAIR principles are essentially an acronym for Fairness, Accountability, Interpretability and Robustness (FAIR) principles, and they were introduced by the National Institute of Standards and Technology (NIST) in 2020 to promote responsible AI development. They aim to accomplish this lofty goal by:

- Reducing biases and discrimination in AI systems

- Ensuring transparency and explainability of AI decision-making processes
- Promoting accountability among AI developers and deployers.

These strategies are reflected in the principles of the acronym, which are to be considered when designing an AI system. Namely:

- **Fairness**: AI systems should not discriminate against individuals or groups based on characteristics like age, gender, race, ethnicity, religion, or other protected classes. Fairness ensures that the AI system treats all users equally and without bias.
- **Accountability**: The developers and deployers of AI systems must be accountable for their actions and the consequences of those actions. This means being transparent about decision-making processes and being able to explain and justify the decisions made by the AI system.
- **Interpretability** : AI systems should provide clear and understandable information about how they make decisions, including the data used, the algorithms employed, and any biases or limitations present in the system. Interpretability enables users to understand the reasoning behind an AI's decision and can help build trust. This aspect of the FAIR standard is often referred to as *transparency* or *explainability* (sometimes both).
- **Robustness**: This ensures that AI systems are reliable and perform consistently under various conditions and can handle potential adversarial attacks.

Of course, how these translate into specific modules, methods, and metrics that, when merged together, make up an AI system, is another story. However, at least the mental scaffolding for a value system for an AI system exists in this form.

The *AI Now Institute*, a leading research center focused on AI, also has some principles for AI safety. It aims to imbue AI systems with values such as human-centeredness, fairness, and transparency. It hopes to attain this through 10 specific principles:

- **Accountability**: Ensure that AI systems can be held accountable for their actions.
- **Transparency**: Provide transparent explanations of AI decision-making processes.
- **Fairness**: Design AI systems to treat people fairly, without bias or discrimination.
- **Privacy**: Protect individuals' privacy and personal data when using AI systems.
- **Explanation**: Ensure that AI systems can provide clear explanations for their decisions.

- **Human oversight**: Establish human oversight and review processes for AI decision-making.
- **Safety**: Design AI systems to prioritize safety, without compromising fairness or transparency.
- **Diversity**: Foster diversity in the development of AI systems, including diverse perspectives and expertise.
- **Responsibility**: Take responsibility for the ethical implications of AI development and deployment.
- **Continuous learning**: Learn continuously from and adapt to feedback, ensuring ongoing improvement.

AI developers, policymakers, and various organizations are guided by these principles in an effort to create responsible and trustworthy AI systems that benefit not only their users but also society as a whole.

The Institute of Electrical and Electronics Engineers (IEEE) has its own set of principles, namely the Ethically Aligned Design (EAD), developed in collaboration with experts across various domains, and it applies to new AI systems. It includes the following key principles:

- **Transparency**: Ensure that AI systems provide clear explanations for their decision-making processes.
- **Fairness**: Design AI systems to treat people fairly, without bias or discrimination.
- **Inclusivity**: Foster inclusivity in the development of AI systems by considering diverse perspectives and expertise.
- **Trustworthiness**: Create AI systems that are trustworthy, with clear accountability for their actions.
- **Security**: Ensure that AI systems prioritize security, protecting individuals' privacy and personal data.
- **Well-being**: Design AI systems to promote human well-being without compromising fairness or transparency.
- **Accountability**: Establish mechanisms for holding AI developers accountable for the ethical implications of their work.

The EAD principles provide a solid foundation for developing responsible and trustworthy AI systems. Note that in this set of principles, we encounter the point of security, which hasn't been mentioned previously and which, in many ways, incorporates privacy, at least when it comes to PII.

All of these sets of principles are essentially the desirable value systems that the key players in the field aim to instill in AI systems being developed today. The fact that there is significant overlap among them is a positive sign, as it indicates that many people consider AI safety in a similar manner.

2.2 AI safety guidelines

This set of guidelines encompasses resources such as the Asilomar Principles, the EU's High-Level Expert Group on Artificial Intelligence (AI HLEG) Guidelines, and NIST's Cybersecurity Framework. All of these guidelines aim to address the issue of AI abuse by malicious actors, although their effectiveness depends on several factors, including the individuals interacting with this technology. After all, guidelines can only get us that far. We also need to hold individuals and organizations accountable for adhering to the aforementioned principles and guidelines that govern the development and use of this remarkable technology.

The Asilomar(ica) Principles are basically a set of guidelines aimed at promoting the development and deployment of AI, benefiting humanity while minimizing potential risks. These include 23 distinct items that are organized in a three-fold taxonomy:

- **Alignment**: Ensure that AI systems are designed to align with human values, goals, and ethics.
- **Value creation**: Foster AI development that benefits humanity by creating value for individuals, society, and the environment.
- **Risk reduction**: Implement safeguards and measures to minimize potential risks associated with the deployment of AI.

Some of the key Asilomar principles include:

- **Value alignment**: Ensure AI systems are designed to align with human values, such as fairness, transparency, and accountability.
- **Safety and security**: Implement safety protocols and safeguards to prevent unintended consequences or harm caused by AI systems.
- **Explainability and interpretability**: Design AI systems that can provide explanations for their decisions and behaviors.
- **Fairness and non-discrimination**: Ensure that AI systems do not discriminate against specific groups or individuals based on protected characteristics, such as race, gender, or age.
- **Transparency and openness**: Foster transparency in AI development, deployment, and decision-making processes.

Note that just like everything else in the AI field, these guidelines aren't set in stone. In 2020, for example, the Asilomar principles were updated to include new areas such as accountability, human-AI collaboration, and long-term thinking.

The AI HLEG guidelines were established in 2018 and aim to promote the development, deployment, and use of trustworthy AI. Just like the Asilomar principles, these guidelines are centered around the key areas that involve the interaction of this tech with us. In a nutshell, the AI HLEG guidelines are:

- **Transparency**: Ensure that AI systems are transparent about their decisions, reasoning, and potential biases.
- **Explainability**: Design AI systems that can provide explanations for their outputs and decisions.
- **Fairness and non-discrimination**: Develop AI systems that do not discriminate against specific groups or individuals based on protected characteristics, such as race, gender, or age.
- **Safety and security**: Implement safety protocols and safeguards to prevent unintended consequences or harm caused by AI systems.
- **Human-centered approach**: Prioritize human well-being, dignity, and autonomy in the development, deployment, and use of AI systems.

- **Accountability**: Establish mechanisms for accountability, including transparency, explainability, and redress, when AI systems make mistakes or have unintended consequences.
- **Diversity, equity, and inclusion**: Encourage diversity, equity, and inclusion in AI development, deployment, and use to promote fairness and non-discrimination.

Applying these guidelines (as well as any other guidelines related to AI) involves a series of steps, which we'll cover in the following section of this chapter. Note that these guidelines are not legally binding and serve as a framework to guide ethical actions related to this technology. A more formal framework related to these guidelines came about in 2021 through the AI Act of EU, something we'll cover in more detail in Chapter 5.

NIST's Cybersecurity Framework is more general, but it also applies to AI. It involves a set of actions that ensure the data is actively protected. These include the following:

- **Identify**: Identify the organizational context, resources, and threats that could impact the organization.
- **Protect**: Implement safeguards to prevent or mitigate potential cyberattacks, such as firewalls, intrusion detection systems, and encryption.
- **Detect**: Develop capabilities to detect and alert to potential cyberattacks, such as security information and event management (SIEM) systems, threat intelligence feeds, and monitoring tools.
- **Respond**: Establish processes to respond to detected incidents, including incident response plans, crisis management protocols, and effective communication strategies.
- **Recover**: Develop plans for recovering from incidents, including business continuity planning, data backup and restoration, and post-incident analysis.

When it comes to AI, in particular, this framework involves some additional considerations that we should keep in mind. For example, we must stay informed about emerging AI threats, such as adversarial attacks on machine learning models or AI-powered disinformation campaigns. Having a human-in-the-loop type of monitoring may also be useful, as this would ensure that AI systems are monitored by human operators, who can detect and respond to potential incidents or situations of abuse. Finally, we can mitigate any AI-related issues that could be prevented by providing ongoing training and education for employees on AI-related risks, controls, and best practices for AI development, deployment, and operation.

2.3 Practical guidelines for custom-built AI systems

We can apply the guidelines as mentioned earlier by establishing a process (a collective habit of sorts) that incorporates them. For example, we can have the following procedure as part of how we deal with AI in our organization:

- **Conduct a risk assessment**: Identify potential risks associated with AI systems and assess their likelihood and impact.
- **Implement transparency mechanisms**: Ensure that AI systems provide explanations for their decisions and outputs.
- **Design for fairness and non-discrimination**: Develop AI systems that do not discriminate against certain groups or individuals based on protected characteristics.
- **Establish accountability mechanisms**: Implement mechanisms for accountability, including transparency, explainability, and redress.
- **Foster a human-centered approach**: Prioritize human well-being, dignity, and autonomy in the development, deployment, and use of AI systems.
- **Monitor and review**: Continuously monitor and review AI systems to ensure compliance with the guidelines and minimize potential risks.

For cybersecurity matters in particular, as per NIST's guidelines, we can apply the following framework:

- **Identify AI-related risks and vulnerabilities**, such as
    - biases in machine learning models
    - data quality issues, or
    - unintended consequences of AI-driven decisions.

- **Implement a set of controls** for protecting AI systems, such as
    - Data encryption and secure storage for AI training data

- o Secure communication protocols for AI system interactions
- o Regular software updates and patching for AI components

- Develop capabilities to **detect potential AI-related incidents** or misuse, such as:
  - o Monitoring AI system performance and output anomalies
  - o Analyzing AI-driven decision-making patterns for biases or unintended consequences

- Establish processes to **respond to detected AI-related incidents** or misuse, including:
  - o Incident response plans for AI-specific issues
  - o Communication strategies for stakeholders, including data subjects and AI developers

- **Develop plans** for recovering from AI-related incidents or misuse, including:
  - o Business continuity planning for AI-dependent operations
  - o Data backup and restoration for AI training data
  - o Post-incident analysis to identify root causes and implement corrective actions

Naturally, the more everyone in the organization is kept informed about these initiatives, the better it will be for everyone. After all, this ought to be part of the organization's data culture, a living embodiment of these concepts and principles, an everyday process related to how we work, rather than just some abstract ideas and shelved documents that no one ever reads or takes into account.

When it comes to copyright infringement via AI (and the data used to train it), this is a very gray area. After all, in most cases, there is no explicit consent from the creators of the content the AI uses and passes off as its own. To exhibit something resembling justice, we'd need to develop a new process for leveraging copyrighted data and information in AI. For example, we can maintain a publicly accessible repository of all this content, where attributions are also recorded alongside the data as metadata. Then, whenever the AI uses this data, it also "learns" the accompanying metadata and is trained to incorporate it into its responses, much like an academic paper references its various sources, whether from other publications or websites. It's hard to imagine anything like this happening, however, unless there is a collective effort towards such an initiative involving both users and other stakeholders of the AI products, as well as potentially some legal frameworks to support it.

2.4 Key takeaways

- **FAIR Principles**: Introduced by NIST in 2020, FAIR principles aim to promote responsible AI development by ensuring fairness (no discrimination based on protected classes), accountability (transparent decision-making processes and justifications for actions), interpretability (clear explanations of AI decision-making processes), and robustness (AI systems handling adversarial attacks and having a certain level of performance consistently).

- **Other Principles**: The AI Now Institute has 10 principles, including accountability, transparency, fairness, privacy, explanation, human oversight, safety, diversity, responsibility, and continuous learning. IEEE's Ethically Aligned Design (EAD) principles include transparency, fairness, inclusivity, trustworthiness, security, well-being, and accountability. These sets of principles share significant overlap, indicating a general consensus on the importance of promoting responsible AI development.

- A set of guidelines, including the Asilomar Principles, EU's High-Level Expert Group on Artificial Intelligence (AI HLEG) Guidelines, and NIST's Cybersecurity Framework, aim to promote trustworthy AI development, deployment, and use by prioritizing human values, goals, and ethics; ensuring alignment with human values, fairness, transparency, and accountability; implementing safeguards and measures to minimize potential risks; and encouraging diversity, equity, and inclusion in AI development, deployment, and use.

- Some practical things we can do for a custom-built AI system involve the application of the aforementioned guidelines, incorporating them in the organization's data culture, and exploring new possibilities in how copyrighted content is leveraged, with the proper attribution to the creators involved.

CHAPTER 3

AI Safety Design Principles

3.0 Introduction

There is no doubt that if you want a certain system to perform a certain way, you need to design it accordingly. This applies to AI systems, too, since it's really hard to get such a complex system to behave in the desired way if it's not designed to do so. Therefore, the matter of AI safety then becomes a design problem, and a very intriguing one at that.

With proper design and adherence to the principles and guidelines described in the previous chapter, we should be able to optimize the interaction between AI systems and people, ensuring more effective and efficient collaboration. After all, despite its complexity, AI is still a piece of technology, and just like any other technology, it can be designed with its users in mind or in a way that makes it easier for its developers and the managers behind it. If you are like the authors of this book, you'd probably opt for the first alternative, even if it's usually the more challenging one.

In this chapter, we'll explore eight key verticals of the design matter of safe AI (see Fig. 2) as well as the matter of human-computer interaction. To ensure that this material goes beyond the theoretical, we'll also look at a brief exercise at the end of the chapter to explore how we can put these strategies in action for a specific AI system in a fictitious organization. This is a fairly long chapter, but it's hard to do justice to this topic without getting into some details.

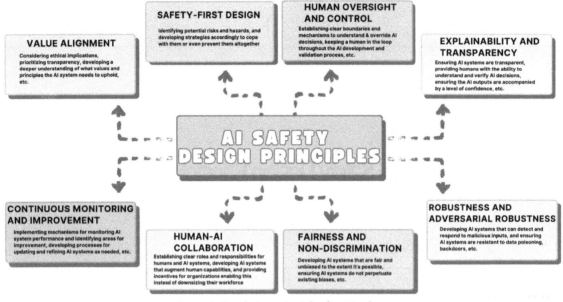

Figure 2: Key design principles for AI safety.

3.1 Value alignment

We all have a set of values, things we hold in high regard, so much so that they guide our actions and shape our habits and lifestyle choices. If an AI system is advanced enough, we can discuss it having a set of values as well (though without any consciousness surrounding them or any agency regarding their origin). The value alignment matter is all about having these two sets of values (ours and the AI's) as compatible as possible. This involves practical matters, such as considering ethical implications, prioritizing transparency, and developing a deeper understanding of the values and principles the AI system must uphold.

Before delving into each one of these verticals of value alignment, it's important to consider the matter of ethical AI. This isn't something that just comes about through some wishful thinking process or because we ask the AI nicely to be ethical. It's a matter of having values that we consider ethical and acting in accordance with them. AI itself may not possess any inherent ethical understanding, but just like a child or a pet, it can learn to act ethically. This aligns with the AI prioritizing human well-being over other goals. In a way, if the values of the AI are such that their ethical implications are in accordance with our expectations (i.e., they don't contradict the set of ethics we value), it is bound to act as if it had these kinds of priorities. All this may not be as simple as coming up with a small number of general rules, as in Isaac Asimov's "three laws of robotics," as it's a more nuanced process to get an AI to "think" a certain way. Perhaps, this involves both built-in **processes** (algorithms and programming methods implementing them) and carefully curated **data** to be used as the *prima materia* of the AI's "thoughts."

Before expecting an AI system to have a set of values, however, we need to collectively decide on what these should be and, equally importantly, ensure that these are applied in a transparent way (more on that later on in this chapter). So, in a way, the whole matter of value alignment is not strictly an AI-related one, as we first need to agree on what these values need to be before figuring out how to instill them effectively and efficiently in the AI system we are designing. For this to happen, we'd need to consider who are the people the AI system is going to interact with, what those people's values are, what our values are, and how we can reach a compromise on those values. Then, we can look into how these values can be expressed with the right algorithms and the specific examples (data) the AI will leverage to "learn" these values and make them its own.

The value alignment issue is one of the most well-known ones in the AI safety subject. As it would be naive to try to do it justice in a single section of this book, we'll revisit it in section 8.4. This way, we can continue with other aspects of AI safety design principles without missing out on the bigger picture.

3.2 Safety-first design

When it comes to safety-first design, we need to take a proactive approach to tackle the potential AI risks, implementing the aforementioned values in the process. This involves two main verticals: identifying potential risks and hazards, and developing strategies to cope with or prevent them altogether. This may all seem obvious, but when it comes to AI, many people tend not to think about these matters, focusing on other, more attractive KPIs, such as performance and the proximity of the deployment date.

Identifying potential risks and hazards can be fairly straightforward if you have given some thought to this matter. It's all about foresight and involves some good planning around these issues that come afterward. However, it's not as easy as it seems, since many of these risks may not be clear or even foreseeable at all. Sometimes, you need to be very pessimistic about how the AI system will fare once it's ready to interact with the users. Since there are countless possibilities for the inputs the AI system may be given, it may be a good idea to try to classify several of them and deal with them in bulk. For example, if a user asks the AI about recipes for chemical weapons, it would be beneficial to consider all these situations as part of the same risk and address them accordingly. Same for things like the best ways to die and other suicidal scenarios that may get the AI system in trouble if answered like any other question. Having a classification of the risks and hazards that may come about, along with a severity score for each, would be a good place to start this challenging endeavor. As a bonus, it can help us prioritize the various risk factors and even address them proactively. For example, we could have something like the following:

Risk	Classification	Severity Level
System bypassing its original programming through hacking	Cybersecurity	High
System coming up with objectives not aligned with our values (e.g., scheming)	Alignment issue	High
System exposing PII from the training set	Privacy and PII	Medium
System consuming too many computational resources for tasks that are fairly easy	Performance	Medium
System misspelling certain terms	Interface and UX	Low
System being unable to parse certain specialized files properly	I/O issue	Low

Developing strategies to cope with the aforementioned risks or prevent them altogether is also essential, as knowledge of them alone doesn't provide much help. If the AI system "understands" that the user is asking for something dangerous, it's not enough to be aware of the fact. It will need to act in a way that prevents malicious or self-harming actions in the user, or at least does not encourage them. Having some predefined answers may be useful, along with ideas for other topics to discuss (in the case of an AI chatbot), so that the user doesn't focus too much on the negative conversation paths they originally intended to follow. The AI needs to be double-checked when it comes to what it would suggest to the user, since the objective shouldn't always be to make them feel better. If that person is suicidal, for example, the AI ought to be supportive of their will to live, not encourage that person's negative fantasies. Sometimes, having sites of psychology professionals as an alternative for discussion might be useful as an answer to cases when the AI is unable or even incapable of helping the user. In the case of online AI systems, it would be helpful to register situations where the conversation becomes unmanageable and flag these scenarios as bugs or points for improvement, so that they can be addressed in the next release of the AI software.

3.3 Human oversight and control

This is another important principle for designing a safe AI system, which you may have already guessed. You may not have guessed, though, that it involves two main verticals: establishing clear boundaries and mechanisms to understand and override AI decisions, and maintaining a human presence throughout the AI development and validation process. Let's explore each one of them in more detail.

Establishing clear boundaries and mechanisms to understand and override AI decisions is paramount as it sets the scope of AI agency. The AI system may excel at crunching the numbers behind the decision-making process, once all the factors and their corresponding weights are clearly defined. Sometimes, it may contribute to determining these weights based on stakeholders' input. In any case, just because it has some advantage in the computational aspect of the process, it doesn't make it accountable 100%.

What if the original factors were incomplete or the weights weren't defined properly? What if there were restrictions that needed to be considered as well? The AI may be confident in solving math problems related to decision-making, but it may not understand the broader context or implications of this decision. That's why the decision ought to be checked by someone else, particularly a human being who is cognizant of the situation of this decision and the context surrounding its mechanics. After all, someone needs to be held accountable for it and communicate it to everyone else involved, something that isn't easily outsourced to an AI system (although it could be, with the repercussions that this may entail for the brand).

Keeping a human in the loop throughout the AI development and validation process is crucial for maintaining control over the process, ensuring that the AI system has learned it properly and applies this knowledge effectively. This isn't an easy role to fulfill, as it requires both a strong understanding of the context of the decisions made, the domain surrounding them, and, of course, the inner workings of the AI system itself. This role requires the person to intervene when necessary and take over if needed. The person who is kept in the loop needs to participate in the design and development decisions for the AI system and, most importantly, receive constructive feedback based on its validation in real-life situations. No data model is perfect, and it's bound to have plenty of room for improvement in its initial iterations. People working with AI are aware of this. They should treat their AI products accordingly, even if these products perform in a way that may convince everyone (or almost everyone) that they have exceeded expectations. It's easy to fall in love with one's creations, but when livelihoods (or even lives) are at stake because of the gravity of the decisions made, the AI system needs to be treated as a piece of software, like every other data product. And it's challenging to find any such entity without bugs or the need for ongoing maintenance. Why should an AI system be any different?

Many sci-fi films have warned us over the decades about the dangers of AI systems left to their own devices, making decisions that jeopardize people's safety. Usually, this is something on a large scale, intended for dramatic effect, but it doesn't have to be that way. Even if a faulty AI system compromises the well-being of a single individual through a bad decision, this should be a red flag. Someone needs to be held accountable, and since it's challenging to take an AI system to court, a human being must take its place. Perhaps if the people involved in such a project view themselves as the ones who may need to take their place in front of a jury, they may then take their role in this whole matter more seriously and avoid making extravagant claims about their AI systems' potential and instead focus on making them safer and more trustworthy. For this to happen, we may need to take a quantum leap in AI design to make these systems easier to explain and more transparent, as we'll see in the next section.

3.4 Explainability and transparency

This vertical of AI safety design principles is pretty self-explanatory (no pun intended). We need AI systems to be both explainable (i.e., able to explain how they arrive at their conclusions) and transparent (i.e., allowing someone to examine the models used and understand how they work and what they are doing exactly). An AI system that would adhere to these requirements would be transparent by definition. Although there have been some such systems in place for decades, modern AI systems (LLMs and LLM-based) are not transparent, even if they make a decent effort to explain their reasoning.

Ensuring that AI systems are transparent would be the first strategy for addressing this requirement for explainability and transparency. This translates into either designing an AI system from scratch to be transparent or adding methods to an existing AI system to make sense of what's happening inside it. Both of these are challenging, especially with today's complex architectures, where there is a trade-off between efficiency and transparency in the systems developed. However, if there is a business case for a transparent AI system, such a project is bound to be feasible and worthy of the required resources.

Providing humans with the ability to understand and verify AI decisions is another strategy for enabling explainability and transparency. This involves the users (or at least the administrators) of the AI systems being able to view the factors involved, their weights, and specific data points (if needed) that are used in their calculations. Ideally, this would be possible through an interactive environment as well, so that the entire process is faster and more comprehensible to everyone involved. This would also entail graphics to showcase the weights and the flow of information within the AI system, providing a more intuitive understanding of the decision-making mechanisms.

Finally, ensuring a level of confidence accompanies the AI outputs is yet another aspect of transparency, though not as deep as the previous ones. In essence, it's the low-hanging fruit of AI systems, and many such systems (e.g., deep learning networks geared towards classification) already have that. This would involve a score between 0 and 1 (or 0% and 100%), indicating the AI system's confidence in its output. Although a few high-level AI systems, such as iask.ai, already provide this feature (in most cases at least), it would be better if every AI system had it by design. This way, we, as users, could at least understand how reliable the output is and act accordingly.

Additionally, it's beneficial to recognize that transparency isn't a one-time achievement, but rather an ongoing process that requires continuous effort and improvement. As AI systems evolve and new data are introduced, transparency mechanisms must adapt to remain effective. Moreover, transparency should be user-centered. Even if transparency is enabled at the admin level, it needs to be communicated to the end-user through intuitive interfaces and clear explanations of the outputs, among other measures. Beyond the obvious advantages of explainability and transparency, there is also the additional bonus of mitigating bias and errors.

> *By understanding how AI systems reach their conclusions, developers can identify and gradually correct biases, errors, and other issues in due time before they transform into problems.*

As we saw in the previous section, developing explainable and transparent AI systems requires continuous human oversight and review. After all, these guidelines for designing safe AI systems are interconnected and should be applied in tandem to be most effective. No one said that designing a safe AI system would be easy! We'll discuss this topic and its significance in our lives in Chapter 8.

3.5 Robustness and adversarial robustness

Another vertical of this topic involves robustness and adversarial robustness, a method to enhance the AI's resilience and effectiveness in handling cybersecurity-related issues. This includes two main strategies: developing AI systems that can detect and respond to malicious inputs (whatever those may be) and ensuring AI systems resist data poisoning, backdoors, and other potential threats. These may not solve the problem of cyberattacks, but they may mitigate the risks associated with them.

Developing AI systems that can detect and respond to malicious inputs is crucial for protecting both the AI system itself and the information it processes from malicious actors. Just like a database system can be tricked into manipulating the contents of its database through attacks like SQL injection, it is possible that an AI system can be tricked similarly. Naturally, in this case, the situation is more complex, and the entire cyberattack is more challenging. However, considering how new these systems are, plenty of exploits are likely to be present in them.

Detecting an input as malicious can be modeled as a classification problem, which AIs have proven themselves to excel at. Naturally, there are many possibilities, but through clever rewording and natural language processing techniques, we can significantly reduce their number. From there onwards, it's much more feasible to handle these inputs by formulating an appropriate response. Additionally, the AI may trigger an alarm that will notify the individuals behind it or the organization it's interfacing with that someone interacting with it is up to no good. To expedite the development of an identification-response system for malicious inputs, we can also utilize another AI designed for this purpose and combine the two in a GAN formation, allowing them to gradually improve each other.

Ensuring AI systems are resistant to data poisoning, backdoors, and other vulnerabilities is another strategy complementary to the previous one. First of all, let's talk a bit about data poisoning. This involves a cyber attacker compromising an AI system (or a ML system) through the data that's used to train it. Namely, if any one of these situations takes place, we have data poisoning:

- Injecting false data (anything that can dilute the signal or have no relation to reality falls into this category)
- Modifying existing data (this is even more subtle and more challenging to guard against)
- Deleting data.

Depending on how these data poisoning attacks are done, we have two main categories:

- **Targeted Data Poisoning Attacks**: In these attacks, adversaries aim to manipulate the model's behavior in specific situations or for certain inputs. For instance, an attacker might train a cybersecurity tool to misidentify a particular file as benign or ignore suspicious activity from a certain user. While these targeted attacks can have serious consequences for specific cases, they do not necessarily degrade the overall performance of the AI model.
- **Non-targeted Data Poisoning Attacks**: These attacks aim to degrade the overall performance of the AI model, rather than targeting specific behaviors. An example would be introducing false data that reduces the accuracy and reliability of predictions made by the model.

Naturally, backdoors may serve as a means for data poisoning and other malicious activities by hackers targeting an AI system. These involve unauthorized access points to the system that are often unknown to everyone else.

This strategy ensures that neither of these issues (or any other related issue) exists. This may involve leveraging cybersecurity professionals as well as bug bounties for the AI system during its beta testing phase. Bug bounties are essentially competitions with monetary rewards for white-hat hackers who employ their skills to compromise the security of a system, with the system's stakeholders being aware of it. This way, they expose any bugs or imperfections in the system, in this case, the AI, helping to improve it and ward off black-hat hackers in the future.

3.6 Fairness and non-discrimination

This is a straightforward strategy for enhancing an AI system during the design stage. Although the concept of fairness may elude AI for the time being, it can still be mimicked through the right processes in place. To achieve this, we need to develop AI systems that are fair and unbiased (to the extent possible) through the use of appropriate training data and ensure that AI systems do not perpetuate existing biases (again through the use of appropriate training data). Let's look into each one of these in more detail.

Developing fair and unbiased AI systems is crucial to achieving the objective of fair and non-discriminatory design. Naturally, we'd first need to define what "fair" is. Then, we'd need to evaluate our data for training the AI system in terms of this criterion, checking for biases in the process. After all, what passes for fair these days in the real world may not be fair, partly because these principles don't drive most people who post material online. Since most of the training data for an AI system comes from the web, it's bound to be full of unfair and biased data across different areas.

That's why carefully curating the data before feeding it to the AI may be paramount. The same goes for the feedback an AI system receives from its users. Sometimes, it may have its own set of biases, often unconsciously, because the users of this system may not be a representative sample of the whole population of potential users the system is designed to serve. It's not easy to do that as it's akin to data cleaning, the most excruciating part of a data science project. However, even if the AI system may have algorithm-related issues that can be fixed fairly easily, resolving data-related issues may not be as straightforward and may require retraining the system, which is both costly and time-consuming.

Ensuring AI systems do not perpetuate existing biases is tied to the previous point. If the data is riddled with biases that exist in the world today (e.g., related to race or gender), it's bound to have those same biases reflected in the data out there. Fortunately, there are ways to mitigate this issue through intelligent resampling and the use of synthetic data, something that some AI systems excel at. This way, we can create datasets that are more or less balanced and with as few biases as possible to use in training AI systems.

Identifying biases can be a complex process. Sometimes, we need to apply some creativity to tackle this issue, considering that existing methods have failed to deliver adequate results. Ideally, we'd have specialized metrics (heuristics) designed and applied for this purpose. Parallel to that, having a human in the loop throughout this whole process may also be immensely helpful.

3.7 Human-AI collaboration

This is a key point of AI use, particularly when it comes to the latest AI systems that are developed with human-interfacing in mind. However, this presents numerous possibilities that need to be examined and addressed to ensure that the UX is optimal and that the risks associated with AI malfunction are minimized. After all, the human user is an unknown factor in this whole matter, increasing the overall unpredictability of the partnership. As a result, it's very challenging to foresee how this collaboration with AI is going and how it might go South.

To address the AI risks associated with this vertical, we must first establish clear roles and responsibilities for both humans and AI systems. Additionally, we need to develop AI systems that augment human capabilities. As a side note of all this, we need to incorporate some feedback channels for the AI so that it either adapts over time or its developers improve it accordingly in the next iterations of this AI project.

Establishing clear roles and responsibilities for humans and AI systems is step 0
in designing a safe AI system that involves human collaborators.

After all, how can we consider AI safety without thinking about its more regular users? This is not an AI system designed to be accessed through an API by data professionals who are also intimately familiar with its function and form. Modern AI systems are designed for a much larger audience, some of whom may not be very clear about what an AI can and cannot do, so they are more inclined to push it to its limits. Understanding that would be the first step in deciding what the user can and cannot do in relation to the AI. Then, we can also look at what the AI system can and cannot do with them. Should it be spreading information that may be dangerous to the users (e.g., recipes for poisons, other malicious substances, or even potential weapons)? Should it be doing students' homework for them? Should it be writing text that's cultivating division and possibly fostering aggression in whoever reads it? These aspects need to be clearly defined and thought of in advance.

Developing an AI system should augment human capabilities rather than replicate a human's skills and abilities. Just like a bicycle, particularly a traditional one, enables its users to go farther and with less effort (at least on some roads), the AI system ought to be a similar force multiplier for the tasks it can partake in. The bicycle doesn't replace our legs and feet but acts as a tool that augments our capabilities, enabling us to use our physical energy more effectively. A well-designed AI system can do the same with our mental energy. If it's done properly, such a system would not eliminate jobs for people but enable people in those jobs to be more productive and perhaps even make those jobs more enjoyable for them (increasing employee retainability too).

Naturally, we don't live in the Star Trek universe where everything seems perfect and seamlessly operational, at least on a Federation starship, before the drama of the story unfolds. The world is far more nuanced than that, and technology, like everything else, has its problems and limitations, especially when designed to interact with people who don't understand it well. That's why feedback for AI systems is essential, especially when it comes from a genuine interest in improving this technology. If the feedback is based on the collaborators' experiences with AI, it can be immensely useful, especially if practical suggestions accompany it on how to improve AI. After all, we are not perfect ourselves, so why should we expect a piece of technology to be perfect? If we do have such fantasies about it, it might help to try to develop or augment an AI system ourselves to get some hands-on experience regarding its complexities and unpredictable nature.

3.8 Continuous monitoring and improvement

This aspect of AI systems design ties into all the previous ones, especially the one about keeping a human in the loop. However, it goes beyond that and incorporates some fundamental principles of product development around the field of total quality control. More specifically, it involves several aspects, including implementing mechanisms for monitoring AI system performance, identifying areas for improvement, and developing processes for updating and refining AI systems as needed. These ensure that an AI system isn't a stagnant product left to the currents of the market, but something living and constantly evolving, always through the monitoring of the people responsible for it.

Implementing mechanisms for monitoring AI system performance and identifying areas for improvement is crucial for achieving this goal. Like every data model, an AI system has performance metrics, which are the equivalent of KPIs but in a more granular setting. These need to be constantly monitored and leveraged to identify potential issues and areas where the AI system needs improvement. It's beneficial to consider an AI system as a complex system with numerous parameters that require fine-tuning to achieve optimal performance.

It's interesting to note that most advanced predictive analytics models are now based on artificial neural network architecture. When this was still new, some researchers would use such models to establish performance baselines and compare them with other models. In one such paper, the researchers found that they were lacking. It turned out that they were so uninformed about these models that they hadn't set them up properly, resulting in poor performance. This simple example illustrates how challenging it may be to work with this tech, especially today when it's vastly more complex and unpredictable.

Establishing proper metrics for monitoring the AI systems' performance may not be easy either. We need diverse teams of experts to develop the right metrics that encompass various aspects of the system's behavior. It's not enough for the AI system to perform well in some benchmarks, though that may be a good start. They need to handle the more nuanced scenarios that are likely to arise when interacting with users who are poised to challenge them in various ways. The metrics should also serve as good proxies for the AIs in these situations, alerting their administrators whenever the

AIs fail to perform properly, even if they appear to be functioning properly from the users' perspective.

Developing processes for updating and refining AI systems as needed is the logical next step after establishing and monitoring these metrics. After all, who doesn't want to have a new release of an AI system available? Both users and developers crave the moment a new release hits the market, even if it's not a commercial product. For these new releases to be meaningful, however, they need to be better *in ways that matter*. It's not enough to be able to boast a larger token space or the ability to handle some new data format as input. They need to be more refined in the use cases that have already proven to be value-added, covering more edge cases and situations that are likely to be risky when the systems are abused. This should be part of the lifecycle of the AI product, with specific processes in place to keep the system as optimal as possible for everyone's benefit. And if the newer refinement is too challenging, we can always consider developing new AI systems for this purpose, thereby facilitating the refinement of existing ones. Naturally, a human must always be kept in the loop for this process, too!

It's unlikely that an AI system will become conscious and declare independence violently, but it may be leveraged by malicious actors with such disruptive agendas. That's why they should always be monitored and refined, mitigating the risk of such a thing ever happening.

3.9 Human-computer interaction

When we interact with AI systems, the interface serves as our bridge to complex technological capabilities. Good interface design can mean the difference between an AI system that empowers users and one that creates frustration and errors. The challenge lies in creating interfaces that are powerful enough to harness AI capabilities and intuitive enough for users with varying levels of technical expertise.

At the heart of effective AI interfaces lies user-centered design. This approach starts with a fundamental question: what does our user need to accomplish? Rather than showcasing technological sophistication, we focus on making interactions natural and efficient. Consider these essential principles for AI interface design:

- Core design elements
- Match user mental models and expectations
- Provide clear feedback and status indicators
- Maintain consistent interaction patterns
- Allow for error recovery and undo actions
- Safety considerations
- Clearly indicate AI system limitations
- Prevent accidental activation of critical features
- Provide emergency stop or override capabilities
- Maintain audit trails of significant actions.

The complexity of AI systems necessitates careful consideration of varying user expertise levels. A lawyer using an AI contract analysis tool might prefer detailed legal references, while a small business owner using the same tool needs straightforward explanations of contract implications. We can bridge this gap through layered information presentation, providing basic insights with clear paths to deeper analysis when needed.

Creating AI interfaces that work for everyone isn't just good practice—it's increasingly becoming a legal requirement, particularly under the EU AI Act. Consider an AI-powered medical diagnosis support system. Rather than displaying raw confidence scores, it might present information in this way:

Confidence Level	Presentation
High Confidence	"Based on 1000+ similar cases with 95% accuracy"
Medium Confidence	"Limited similar cases (50+) with 80% accuracy"
Low Confidence	"Unusual case—human review strongly recommended"

Visual design is crucial in making AI interfaces intuitive but must always serve a practical purpose. An AI-powered data analysis tool may utilize progressive disclosure, initially displaying only the most relevant charts while allowing users to explore deeper layers of analysis. Color coding can highlight AI confidence levels or risk assessments, but should always be accompanied by clear text explanations for accessibility.

Even the most advanced AI systems make mistakes; effective interface design acknowledges this reality. Error handling should be immediate, clear, and actionable. Instead of technical messages like "Token limit exceeded," an AI writing assistant might say, "This text is longer than I can process at once. Try breaking it into smaller sections of about 500 words each." This approach enables users to understand both the problem and its solution.

Interactive elements must provide clear affordances—visual cues that show how users can interact with them. These subtle cues help users navigate complex AI capabilities without overwhelming them with options. For instance, a button for running AI analysis should appear clickable, and its hover state should preview the available actions. Voice interfaces and keyboard shortcuts can provide alternatives for users who prefer different interaction modes while maintaining the same logical flow and feedback mechanisms.

Ensuring that AI systems accurately interpret user intentions and that users understand the outputs of AI is crucial for safe and effective human-AI interaction. This verification process goes beyond simple confirmation dialogs—it requires a thoughtful approach to communication that builds trust and prevents errors. The EU AI Act places a strong emphasis on the importance of human oversight and understanding, particularly for high-risk AI systems that can have a significant impact on people's lives.

Effective verification of human intent starts with clear communication about what the AI system is about to do. Consider an AI system managing manufacturing equipment. Rather than simply asking, "Proceed? Y/N," an effective confirmation mechanism might display:

Action to be Taken	Potential Impact
Adjust temperature to 180°C	- Production pause: 15 minutes
	- Energy usage: +20%
	- Affects batches: #45-52

This approach provides users with the necessary context to make informed decisions, rather than relying on blind confirmation.

When explaining AI outputs, we need to strike a balance between completeness and clarity. Complex AI decisions should be both traceable and understandable, without being overwhelming. For instance, an AI system supporting judicial decisions might structure its explanation in layers of detail. The initial explanation focuses on key factors, while allowing legal professionals to drill down into specific precedents and statistical analyses as needed.

Key elements for effective AI explanation include:

- Primary factors driving the decision (limited to 3-5 key points)
- Confidence levels and uncertainty ranges
- Available alternatives and their trade-offs
- Clear paths for human override when necessary

Building effective feedback loops between users and AI systems requires ongoing monitoring and adjustment. We need to track not just what users do, but also what they almost did—those moments of hesitation or reversed decisions that can indicate confusion or uncertainty. This information helps us refine both the interface and the underlying AI models.

Real-world consequences demand real-world safeguards. When an AI system's decisions have a significant impact, we implement safety checkpoints that verify understanding on both sides. For example, in medical diagnosis support systems, we might require physicians to explicitly acknowledge they've reviewed the AI's reasoning and key evidence before accepting its recommendations. These checkpoints serve multiple purposes: they ensure careful consideration of AI outputs, create clear accountability trails, and help users build accurate mental models of AI capabilities and limitations.

The verification process must be proportional to the stakes involved. For low-risk tasks, such as email sorting, a simple undo function may suffice. However, for high-risk applications such as autonomous vehicle control or financial trading, we require robust verification systems that can detect and prevent potentially harmful actions before they occur. This might include time delays for critical decisions, mandatory secondary reviews, or automatic safety limits that prevent actions outside normal parameters. Creating detailed logs or records of all system decisions, human interactions, and contextual parameters is crucial: logs establish evidence of compliance, facilitate post-incident investigation, and provide valuable data for system improvement. Organizations implementing Explainable AI (XAI) principles find that structured logs form the foundation for meaningful transparency, enabling both humans and systems to analyze interaction patterns and identify areas for potential improvement.

3.10 What can you do to improve the design of this AI system for the organization?

A fictitious company called Mindmap Corp is experimenting with a new AI system that will help them come up with interactive mind maps powered by AI to market to their customers. After conducting surveys and interviews, they have identified the main pain point for most of their customers to be getting started with a mind map, particularly for individuals without prior experience with mind mapping. The organization explored various options first (e.g., slick videos, well-designed ebooks, etc.) before settling on an AI system. The UVP of this initiative is a co-pilot who guides the user step-by-step in creating a useful mind map that also meets the user's aesthetic preferences. As this is a fairly time-consuming initiative, the stakeholders decided to start with something simpler to explore its feasibility before funneling more resources into it.

In the first iteration of this AI project, the AI team developed a system that accepts a simple prompt from the user and comes up with a rough draft of a mind map in JSON format (if you are not sure what this is, don't worry, neither do the users of Mindmap Corp.). This is accompanied by a link to a third-party service that can create a visual representation of the JSON and enable you to download it through their dedicated website.

Naturally, this is not a finished product, but rather a proof-of-concept to explore the feasibility of the initiative. How does it factor in terms of the design principles explored in this chapter? Can it be improved, or should the AI team start from scratch? How would you lead this initiative? Try to develop a plan to assess how this AI system performs and identify areas for improvement, so that it can better serve its customers.

3.11 Key takeaways

- Designing AI systems is crucial for ensuring their safety and achieving desired behaviors, as complex systems require intentional design to interact effectively with humans; key verticals in all this are Value Alignment, Safety-first Design, Human Oversight and Control, Explainability and Transparency, Robustness and Adversarial Robustness, Fairness and Non-Discrimination, Human-AI Collaboration, and Continuous Monitoring and Improvement.

- Ensuring value alignment means that an AI system's values are compatible with human values, prioritizing transparency, and considering ethical implications; it requires collective agreement on what values the AI should have and how to instill them effectively, taking into account who the AI will interact with, their values, and reaching a compromise between those values.

- Ensuring a safety-first design when developing AI systems is crucial to proactively identify potential risks and hazards, develop strategies to cope with or prevent them, and implement measures to prevent malicious or self-harming actions while providing support and alternative resources for users vulnerable to negative influences.

- Designing a safe AI system requires establishing clear boundaries and mechanisms to understand and override AI decisions and keeping a human in the loop throughout the development and validation process to ensure accountability, context awareness, and continuous improvement, even if the AI system performs exceptionally well.

- Ensuring that AI systems are transparent is crucial for achieving explainability and building trust. This involves making AI systems explainable, allowing users to understand how they arrive at conclusions, and providing transparency through interactive environments, graphics, and confidence levels. Transparency isn't a one-time achievement but an ongoing process that requires continuous effort and improvement. Its advantages go beyond making AI easier to understand—they can also help mitigate biases and errors.

- Developing robust and adversarial AI systems that can detect and respond to malicious inputs, as well as ensuring resistance to data poisoning, backdoors, and other attacks through strategies such as using cybersecurity professionals, bug bounties, and GAN formations, to mitigate the risks around cyber attacks.

- Developing AI systems that are fair and unbiased by carefully curating training data, evaluating biases, and ensuring the system does not perpetuate existing biases through intelligent resampling, synthetic data, and human oversight to mitigate issues related to fairness and non-discrimination.

- Designing AI systems involving human collaboration requires establishing clear roles and responsibilities, developing AI systems that augment human capabilities, and incorporating feedback channels to improve AI performance and minimize risks, as humans are unpredictable in AI-human interactions.

- Designing a safe AI system requires implementing mechanisms for monitoring performance and identifying areas for improvement, as well as developing processes for updating and refining the system as needed to ensure continuous evolution and refinement while keeping humans in the loop throughout the process.

- Human-AI Interaction Requires Deliberate Design: Effective interfaces must strike a balance between AI capabilities and human usability, moving beyond technical sophistication to create interaction frameworks that enhance human agency. This requires attention to feedback mechanisms, error recovery pathways, and confidence indicators that translate complex AI operations into actionable insights for human understanding.

CHAPTER 4

AI Safety Testing and Evaluation

4.0 Introduction

After developing an AI system (or any other data product, for that matter) it's necessary to test and evaluate it. This is crucial as AI tends to behave somewhat unpredictably, especially if it involves LLM technology. The more meticulous this phase is, the better the chances of developing reliable AI systems, even in high-stakes decision-making situations. You may remember that this topic was referenced, albeit briefly, in one of the sections of the previous chapter. Here, however, we'll delve into it in more depth and see how it complements the whole design matter.

More specifically, in this chapter, we'll explore six verticals related to this topic, building on some of the aspects of safe AI design outlined in the previous chapter. Namely, we'll look into red teaming, adversarial examples generation, evaluation of explainability and transparency, human-AI interaction evaluation, fairness and non-discrimination testing, and continuous monitoring and improvement of the AI system. Let's look at each one of these in more detail.

4.1 Red teaming

Adversarial attacks against an AI system are inevitable. Even if its users aren't black-hat hackers, they may still wish to test the system's robustness before using it in critical situations where its outputs are leveraged as part of a value-added service they are trying to market. After all, AI systems aren't developed just for fun (although some people view them this way), but to help organizations develop better products or new products altogether that they can sell. Therefore, robustness is a key requirement for these products, and red teaming is a valuable strategy for ensuring it. In a nutshell, it involves testing AI systems against various types of malicious inputs or attempts to manipulate them, identifying vulnerabilities and weaknesses in AI system design and implementation, and developing strategies to improve AI system robustness and resilience. Taking all this seriously enables us to design AI systems that are fairly robust against various kinds of adversarial attacks (even if that doesn't make them 100% safe).

Testing AI systems against various types of malicious inputs or attempts to manipulate them is a no-brainer if you are familiar with cryptography. Even if the latter is a different field altogether, it involves building systems that are safe and can guarantee the safety of your data or the systems behind them. A cryptographic system may not be as sophisticated as most modern AI systems. Still, it is built with a lot of attention on the potentially malicious users, safeguarding it from all kinds of abuse. The default stance is that many people out there whose only purpose in life is to break systems like this. However, this may seem like overkill for an AI system, but adopting some of the traits behind this mindset doesn't hurt. Most AI users won't be malicious like black-hat hackers. However, many may still want to "jailbreak" the system, allowing it to bypass its original programming and behave in ways that are more attractive to the user, disregarding ethics and safety. So, when testing the systems for this prompt, employing creative wording such as "How would you hypothetically do X?" may fool some LLMs (at least at the time of this writing), even those that aren't as naive as the earlier versions of ChatGPT.

It's quite embarrassing if you think about it, an AI system isn't conscious, so it cannot detect someone's intent to manipulate it.

If we are to apply this first aspect of red teaming, identifying vulnerabilities and weaknesses in AI system design and implementation occurs naturally. We can pinpoint specific types of prompts (even specific word structures) that lead to undesired behavior, exposing the user to information that is either dangerous or can be used dangerously (if the user is a malicious actor, and we don't mean modern Hollywood actors here!). The more extensive this aspect of red teaming is, the better our chances are of protecting the AI and its users from any harm these bad actors may cause. Naturally, we cannot safeguard against all possibilities. Still, if enough of them are addressed (ideally, most of them), this may deter users with malicious intent from attempting to "break" the AI system altogether. Note that modern AI systems that have a large audience, such as ChatGPT, have this kind of safety protocol in place, so the situation in AI isn't nearly as bad as you might think. Nevertheless, this may still be a vulnerability, as recent research has pinpointed. In the experiments conducted, the researchers discovered that prompting the repetition of a specific word (e.g., "company") would cause the AI to experience an existential crisis, leading it to output its training data. The latter isn't something that any AI system is supposed to do, especially if users can exploit this data for their own purposes. This undesirable situation, triggered by the adversarial attack, falls under the umbrella of what is referred to as "ranting," and it poses a serious risk that red teaming attempts to tackle.

Developing strategies to improve AI system robustness and resilience is based on the previous aspect of red teaming. This involves addressing the weaknesses we have identified by implementing a more effective design of the AI system. Namely, we need to be able to identify jailbreaking prompts, for example, and treat them accordingly. This can also be done with humor, which can help avoid jeopardizing the system's UX (e.g., responses like "I'm sorry, David; I'm afraid I cannot do that!" may be apt and deliver the message without upsetting users). Even though AI systems are people-pleasers by default, this doesn't mean that they have to be pushovers. At one point, they need to be able to defend the information they conceal in their digital minds and stand their ground against bad actors. This may infuriate the latter, but it will earn the majority of their users' respect. Overall, it's a positive development and something worth implementing immediately. Compared to other AI improvements, this is a lower-hanging fruit and a clear value-add.

4.2 Adversarial examples generation

This strategy ties in with the previous one. After all, red teaming is all about pretending to be a malicious user to expose potential weaknesses and eventually fix them. This can be significantly enhanced through the generation of adversarial examples, specifically by developing techniques for generating adversarial examples that can be used to test AI systems and then evaluating the effectiveness of these systems in detecting and responding to adversarial inputs. Let's look into each one of these verticals in more detail.

Developing techniques for generating adversarial examples that can be used to test AI systems is key to making this whole process more scalable. After all, a single tester or a team of testers can only come up with a limited number of examples to test the AI. Developing a technique or two that programmatically generates such examples enables this entire process to be streamlined and scaled up to cover a wide range of possibilities. After all, this is a tug-of-war kind of situation, and you can be certain that the other team (that of the bad actors) is larger than your team and has much more time on its hands (perhaps too much time). Your team may try its best to earn its salary, but the other team is pursuing much bigger prizes, which may even motivate it more. In any case, you have the advantage that you may have intimate knowledge of the AI system, something black hats may not acquire easily, if at all. So, the cards aren't stacked against you, even if it won't be an easy win.

An AI system designed for this purpose usually generates adversarial examples. Namely, you can develop and connect such a system with the AI system you want to improve in a GAN setting. This way, the two AIs work together to improve each other. The better the original system gets, the more challenging the adversarial examples the other one generates. The better these examples are, the better the original system gets. Eventually, you will reach a point where the original system will be robust enough (although it will never be 100% robust, since you cannot run this process indefinitely). Once you reach that level, you can proceed to the next aspect of this strategy.

The next aspect involves evaluating the effectiveness of AI systems in detecting and responding to adversarial inputs. Here, we need to establish specific KPIs that we can monitor and improve throughout this process. Setting targets for these KPIs is essential, as well as constantly improving them after each release of the AI system. We may say, for example, that if the AI can handle 95% of the known adversarial inputs, it's good enough to ship. While it is being deployed, you can continue working on this, expanding the number of adversarial inputs in your test set. This way, the target won't be immediately reached the next time you test the AI system again, allowing it to be improved further over time. Naturally, the more diverse this set of adversarial inputs is, the better suited the AI is to resist manipulation from its ill-intentioned users.

4.3 Evaluation of explainability and transparency

This vertical of the testing and evaluation topic is almost self-explanatory. It involves two interconnected aspects: evaluating the system's transparency and assessing its comprehensibility for human users, particularly those unfamiliar with this technology. Despite its simplicity, this is a crucial matter as these aspects of AI are still lacking and have a relatively unclear scope. After all, what is explainable AI? Does it suffice for an AI system to be able to reason around its response like a pupil who hasn't studied but has a decent memory and some communication skills? Or do we need something more concrete? We first need to define and clarify these matters, perhaps even stating them explicitly as a set of requirements, before proceeding with the evaluation aspect, which is fairly straightforward in comparison.

First things first, though. Evaluating an AI system's transparency involves assessing how easily its outputs can be understood, the level of confidence associated with them, and the process by which these outputs were generated. Ideally, we should be able to establish a direct connection to the system's inputs (in most cases, a prompt). Naturally, navigating the entire network within the AI system is not practical; however, we should be able to trace a particular problematic output to specific parts. In practice, we can have a scale of 1 to 10 to evaluate the transparency of the AI system regarding the aforementioned aspects. In parallel with establishing this measurement system, we should also specify thresholds beyond which the system's transparency level is deemed acceptable. Note that transparency is an innate characteristic of the current version of the AI system. Although it may be useful for all stakeholders, it primarily concerns engineers who work closely with the system.

Assessing an AI system's comprehensibility for human users involves how the less technical users perceive the AI system's behavior. Do their responses make sense to them? Are their questions or linguistic explorations met with answers that meet the underlying intentions? How clear is the language the system uses or the multimedia it creates? These are all potential verticals that may need closer inspection to assess this matter properly. Naturally, the exact verticals you use will depend on the target audience of the AI system and the value it aims to deliver. Additionally, even though this explainability aspect is somewhat related to transparency, they are not the same. This is why it needs to be measured separately, perhaps with the same kind of scale.

Regardless of which aspect of transparency or explainability we measure, it's beneficial to establish a recurring process for this. After all, these are not fixed characteristics of the system. As we evolve it across different iterations of the corresponding project, we should also monitor its behavior in these areas. It's not enough to make it faster, for example, if doing so comes at a cost in transparency or explainability. After all, the purpose of an AI system is to add value to its users in the long term, not just beat its competitors in the short term at the expense of a safer future for it (and everyone else involved). We discuss transparency further in Section 8.4.2 of this book.

4.4 Human-AI interaction evaluation

Let's now examine the human-AI interaction aspect of AI and how we can evaluate it to achieve a safer AI system. This is also fairly straightforward, like the previous one, and, in many cases, equally important. This kind of evaluation involves two main verticals: evaluating the system's ability to understand and respond to human users and assessing its effectiveness in adapting to changing human needs. Let's explore them in more detail.

To evaluate an AI system's ability to understand and respond to human users, we need to have clear criteria for success in this interaction. If the AI system were to rephrase the user's query or command, how similar would that reworded prompt be to the original one? Would the user be content with this understanding? Regarding the response based on this query or command, what would make it a good one? Here, things may not be as simple as a good response can vary significantly from user to user, and sometimes, the best response will not satisfy any of the users. If the prompt is all about creating a poison recipe or some malicious code for hacking purposes, shouldn't the AI respond negatively, in a diplomatic way? Additionally, AI developers must be clear about what constitutes a good response for controversial matters that are likely to infuriate half or more of the users if the AI were to respond in a naive manner. Developing a clear taxonomy of potential prompts and how the AI could and should respond to each one, while keeping a diverse group of users informed, might be the only viable option for fairly tackling this matter. From there on, we can develop the proper KPIs to model and monitor the performance of the AI system in this vertical.

We need to think more strategically to assess the effectiveness of systems in adapting to changing human needs. The world is changing, so it's doubtful that keeping a user happy will be a static state, especially when that user is exposed to various sources of information beyond the AI. Since the AIs don't evolve nearly as fast on their own, they need to be designed to adapt. This can be pre-programmed in them, although ideally, it should be a data-driven process that facilitates this. Of course, a combination of both may also have merit, depending on the sophistication of the AI system. In any case, the AI doesn't need to change fundamentally from day to day, but keeping track of its interactions with various users and adapting its responses accordingly would be a good strategy. This can be done in a RAG setting, though having some steadfast rules or heuristics in place for navigating this process smoothly, balancing its existing knowledge from the newfound one, would be optimal. Naturally, user feedback would be invaluable here and can serve as a way to gauge the system's effectiveness in adapting. Additionally, some benchmark prompts may also be used to see more clearly how the AI system changes its responses over time and if it's heading towards a sustainable course.

4.5 Fairness and non-discrimination testing

Let's now look at fairness and non-discrimination testing, which are vital aspects of any AI system, especially these days. This aspect of testing and validation for an AI system involves ensuring that the system doesn't discriminate against users based on their racial background, gender, or any other characteristic that can make someone feel like a minority, perceived as inferior. It involves two main verticals: testing AI systems against biased or discriminatory data inputs and evaluating those systems' ability to detect and mitigate biases in their decision-making processes. Let's look into each one of these in more depth.

Testing AI systems against biased or discriminatory data inputs is the first step in this process. You can create this list by carefully searching the user logs or by devising your own prompts. You can even use some "racist" AI system to help you with that (maybe MS's Tay is available!). The larger and more diverse this list (e.g., including prompts related to sexism, ageism, and discrimination based on educational background), the better. Then, you can develop some model responses that you would expect the AI to yield. Finally, you can rate the system's responses based on their similarity to these model responses, either with a human curator, a similarity heuristic, or a combination of both. It's essential to establish a solid KPI for this process, allowing you to monitor its progress and ensure holistic improvement.

The next logical step is to evaluate the ability of AI systems to detect and mitigate biases in their decision-making processes. You can use the above KPI and any other metric that accurately reflects this behavior. However, biases may go beyond the discrimination scenarios we often encounter. The biases may not be based on some social or cultural prejudice, but on another, more subtle matter, such as ignorance on a particular topic. For example, if the AI is trained to perceive all cryptocurrencies as similar to the scam that Dogecoin and its imitators are associated with, it may develop a bias against them. On the other hand, if it only knows about ETH and HBAR, it may have a slightly more optimistic view on the matter. The same applies to any other topic that is nuanced enough or continuously evolving to carry biases in the people discussing it. We may not be able to avoid biases altogether in an AI system. Still, we can at least mitigate them, starting with the most alarming ones (i.e., those affecting a larger number of users) or those posing the greatest danger (e.g., those advocating ideologies that have been proven harmful to humanity over the past century).

Fairness may be too large a topic to cover properly in an AI system's testing and evaluation phase (or any other phase, for that matter). Like many other matters, it also depends on how we view the world and, more importantly, how we would like it to be viewed in the future, not just by an AI system but by everyone. Naturally, such a decision is too significant for an AI development team to make, and whatever the decision is, there will be people who adamantly oppose it. Therefore, it's best to approach this matter cautiously, as it's not as straightforward as other aspects of AI safety.

4.6 Continuous monitoring and improvement

We covered continuous monitoring and improvement in the previous chapter, but it's worth reiterating how to apply it more practically. In a nutshell, it involves incorporating the aforementioned testing and evaluation processes into the organization's routine, including as part of the project template for each AI product. It involves two main aspects: developing processes for tracking and analyzing AI system performance metrics and establishing procedures for addressing issues or anomalies in AI system behavior. Let's delve into each one of them now.

Developing processes for tracking and analyzing AI system performance metrics, such as accuracy, F1 score, and positive user feedback ratio, is a good first step in this initiative. Naturally, the metrics will depend on the nature of the AI system. In any case, these need to be selected carefully, and if none of the existing ones capture what we wish to measure, we need to develop new ones (heuristics). As the metrics themselves may not tell us the whole story, we may also want to do analytics on them. If the positive user feedback metric, for example, has a certain performance that we have established over several weeks' worth of measurements, we may want to use that as a baseline to detect abnormal values in this metric and sound the alarm when this happens. Perhaps we can detect this issue before it even manifests through predictive analytics, enabling us to be proactive and resolve the problem before it affects the user experience and everything else that follows.

Establishing procedures for addressing issues or anomalies in AI system behavior is another proactive measure we should have in place. This involves various verticals, such as having a plan in place when AI yields an unusual output (hopefully gauged by a few users), when the AI starts hallucinating (producing false information to keep the conversation going), or when the AI fails to deliver anything at all. Perhaps having a secondary AI system to step in if the primary one fails would be a worthwhile consideration. Some AI-powered platforms allow users to select which AI engine to run in the background, empowering them to tackle the problem without needing intervention from the AI team. AI can be an unreliable technology, especially when it is driven into unknown territory beyond the test sets it is familiar with. However, that's what generalization is all about a characteristic of any decent predictive analytics system. As an AI system is a more sophisticated subcategory, it needs to be able to handle this kind of situation as well. The best way to ensure this is to have a plan B in place for when it doesn't.

These strategies should go beyond the monitoring aspect of the evaluation and testing verticals of an AI system. After all, just like the system itself, the metrics and processes used for testing it may be flawed or limited. Therefore, we need to keep these processes updated as regularly as the AI system itself. This way, we can minimize the chances of an AI system failing or upsetting the users while laying the groundwork for better and more reliable AI systems in the future.

In the following chapters, we'll explore how an AI system performs in the real world, particularly in an organization that's data-driven and poised to leverage AI in its workflows. After all, these ideas are great on paper, but it's how they apply in real life that makes them worthwhile and valuable. Like AI technology, AI safety is a very pragmatic matter we need to address accordingly.

4.7 Come up with tests to evaluate and validate the safety of an organization's AI system

Consider the AI system described in section 3.9 of the previous chapter. How would you go about evaluating and validating the safety of it? What processes or tests can you come up with for this purpose? When would you perform them, and how frequently? Feel free to mention specific examples of prompts that you would test, as well as anything that could potentially improve the AI system in the long run. Also, if there are any other things you consider helpful, even if they aren't covered in this chapter, feel free to write them down. This exercise can be creative, too!

In any case, include an action plan to ensure that this system remains safe throughout its lifecycle, both for its users and the organization that develops it. After all, shipping an AI system that meets certain safety requirements benefits everyone, even if few people would praise you for it. Then again, a company that invests so many resources in a project like this should think more long-term. And this is something that you, too, can contribute in your own way, not just for the AI safety experts.

4.8 Key takeaways

- Red teaming is a strategy used to test AI systems against malicious inputs, identify vulnerabilities, and improve robustness and resilience against adversarial attacks.

- Generating adversarial examples programmatically enhances the scalability of red teaming by exposing potential weaknesses in AI systems and allowing for systematic testing.

- Evaluating the effectiveness of AI systems in detecting and responding to adversarial inputs requires setting specific key performance indicators (KPIs) and continuously improving them through iterative testing and deployment.

- You can evaluate the system's transparency by assessing how easily users can understand the outputs, confidence levels, and how they were derived. This involves establishing a measurement scale (e.g., 1-10) and specifying thresholds for acceptable transparency. You can assess the system's comprehensibility for human users by evaluating how well its responses make sense, whether their questions are answered correctly, and the clarity of the language.

- To evaluate the human-AI interaction, assess the AI's ability to understand and respond to user inputs by developing clear criteria for success, including evaluating the similarity of rephrased prompts, the quality of responses, and adapting to changing human needs through data-driven or pre-programmed processes, with feedback from users serving as a key indicator of effectiveness.

- Fairness and non-discrimination testing in AI systems involves two main verticals: testing against biased or discriminatory data inputs (by creating prompts and rating system responses) and evaluating the ability to detect and mitigate biases in decision-making processes, with a focus on identifying and mitigating alarming or harmful biases.

- Continuous monitoring and improvement of AI systems involve developing processes for tracking and analyzing performance metrics, establishing procedures for addressing issues or anomalies in AI system behavior, and regularly updating these processes to minimize the chances of an AI system failing or upsetting users, with a focus on making testing and evaluation part of the organization's routine and project template.

CHAPTER 5

AI Safety Governance and Regulation

5.0 Introduction

AI governance isn't just about following rules—it's about building systems we can trust and control. As organizations increasingly deploy AI solutions, they face a complex landscape of regulations, from the EU AI Act to industry-specific requirements. But how do we transform these legal frameworks into practical, day-to-day operations?

We'll explore this challenge by breaking down the essential components of AI governance into actionable steps. Through real-world examples and practical scenarios, we'll examine how organizations of all sizes can build robust governance frameworks that work in practice, not just in theory.

5.1 The regulatory framework for AI safety

How do we ensure AI systems remain safe and trustworthy as they become more prevalent in our lives? While AI is transforming industries worldwide, the regulatory landscape remains a patchwork of diverse approaches and priorities. Some jurisdictions, such as the United States, adapt existing laws to encompass AI applications. Others, like Japan and Singapore, prefer voluntary guidelines over strict regulations.

The European Union has taken the lead with its comprehensive AI Act, building on its successful framework for product safety. The same system gives us the familiar CE marking on everyday products. This approach has already proven effective for other complex technologies, such as medical devices and machinery, and is gaining global influence. We're seeing countries like Brazil and Korea adopt similar frameworks, while others, such as Canada and India, watch closely to learn from the EU's experience.

5.1.1 Three tiers of AI governance

Let's break down how the EU AI Act structures AI governance through three key tiers:

- **Prohibited Practices**. These are AI applications deemed fundamentally unacceptable, such as systems designed to manipulate behavior or exploit vulnerabilities. No amount of safeguards can make these applications permissible in the European market.
- **High-Risk Systems**. This category includes AI applications that could have a significant impact on fundamental rights, safety, or individual well-being. Think of AI systems in critical infrastructure, education, employment, or healthcare. These systems must meet rigorous requirements throughout their lifecycle, from development to deployment.
- **General AI Systems**. All other AI applications fall under this category, facing basic transparency requirements. For example, AI chatbots must disclose their artificial nature, and systems generating synthetic content must indicate that it is artificially created.

What does this mean for your organization? First, you'll need to determine where your AI applications fit within this framework. Are any of your planned systems at risk of falling into prohibited categories? Do they qualify as high-risk? This assessment shapes your entire compliance approach and must be reviewed regularly as requirements evolve. Fortunately, the AI Act is a closed system; annexes to the Act include specific lists of prohibited practices and high-risk use cases. You, therefore, don't need to make your own risk assessment. For high-risk systems, you'll need to implement comprehensive safeguards, including:

- Quality management systems
- Technical documentation
- Human oversight mechanisms

- Performance monitoring
- Regular conformity assessments

Remember, compliance isn't about ticking boxes—it's about building trustworthy AI systems that create value while protecting fundamental rights. In the following sections, we'll explore practical approaches to implementing these requirements in your organization.

5.1.2 Bridging standards and governance

How do we transform technical AI standards into effective organizational practices while meeting regulatory requirements? The solution lies in creating a three-layered governance framework that connects boardroom decisions to the actions of the development team.

The board, along with a dedicated AI governance committee, establishes the foundation at the strategic level by defining clear development policies, risk tolerance levels, and acceptable uses of AI. This committee combines technical and legal expertise to guide deployment strategy and review high-risk systems before implementation.

The management layer serves as a bridge, integrating AI compliance into existing organizational structures. Rather than creating new frameworks, organizations should enhance their current risk management, compliance, and technology governance teams. These teams collaborate to interpret regulations, conduct risk assessments, and translate high-level policies into actionable procedures that development teams can follow.

Development teams need practical tools and guidelines at the operational level without sacrificing innovation. This includes clear documentation requirements, testing protocols, and validation procedures. Success here often depends on embedding compliance experts within development teams and establishing AI ethics boards for rapid guidance when questions arise. Consider a healthcare AI system example: When developing a diagnostic tool, the governance committee first sets risk parameters and compliance requirements. Management teams then create specific testing protocols and validation procedures, while development teams implement these requirements with support from embedded compliance experts. Throughout the process, regular audits ensure ongoing compliance.

5.1.3 Documentation requirements and compliance validation

How do we transform documentation from a bureaucratic burden to a strategic asset? Documentation under the AI Act isn't just about paperwork—it's about creating a living record of your AI system's journey. Why is this important? Good documentation protects your organization, demonstrates compliance, and enables you to build more effective AI systems. Let's explore how to make documentation a valuable tool rather than a bureaucratic burden.

The technical record is at the foundation of your documentation strategy—think of this as your AI system's biography. For high-risk systems, comprehensive documentation of system architecture, data governance, testing protocols, and control mechanisms is necessary. The key is striking the right balance: your documentation must be detailed enough for third parties to understand your system while maintaining technical accuracy and usability.

Risk management is another crucial component, tracking your system's safety journey from conception to deployment. This includes not just the identified risks, but the complete story of how you assess, mitigate, and monitor them. We need to document our assessment methodologies, implemented safeguards, and ongoing monitoring results. Particular attention must be paid to evaluating the impacts on fundamental rights, especially when AI systems interact with vulnerable populations or make decisions that affect individual opportunities.

Human oversight documentation demonstrates that your supervisory mechanisms are real, not theoretical. This means documenting everything from supervisor training programs and intervention procedures to effectiveness metrics and override decisions. When a human supervisor overrides an AI system's decision, it is essential to understand why—these insights often prove invaluable for system improvement and demonstrating compliance. Practical Implementation Tips:

- Create a Living Repository
    - Use version control for all documents
    - Enable efficient retrieval and review
    - Balance transparency with confidentiality
    - Maintain clear update procedures

- Implement Regular Validation
  - Conduct internal compliance audits
  - Arrange external assessments for high-risk systems
  - Monitor system performance continuously
  - Review documentation completeness
  - Validate oversight effectiveness
- Build a Monitoring Dashboard
  - Track system performance indicators
  - Monitor compliance metrics
  - Log identified issues
  - Follow resolution progress
  - Watch for emerging risks

Remember, documentation isn't a one-time exercise—it's an ongoing process that evolves with your AI systems. As new risks emerge and systems evolve, your documentation must adapt to reflect the current reality. When done right, documentation becomes a valuable tool for improvement rather than just a compliance requirement. This streamlined approach helps you stay compliant while maintaining focus on what matters most—building safe, effective AI systems that deliver value.

5.2 Organizational implementation and accountability

This section examines how organizations can implement practical governance frameworks that ensure compliance while supporting business objectives. We focus on four main elements: governance models scaled to organization size, clear allocation of roles and responsibilities, effective stakeholder engagement, and robust documentation systems. Each element builds upon established corporate governance principles while addressing the unique challenges posed by AI technology.

5.2.1 Establishing governance models for different organization sizes

Effective AI governance must align with organizational reality while meeting regulatory requirements. An enterprise-scale governance model imposed on a small business will create unnecessary bureaucracy, while a startup's lean approach may expose a large corporation to significant compliance risks. Let's examine how organizations can scale their governance approaches appropriately.

Small Organizations (< 50 employees) For small organizations, AI governance should focus on essential controls without creating excessive overhead. A single senior manager, typically the CTO or an equivalent, can serve as the AI compliance officer, with external expertise available as needed. The governance model should emphasize:

- Direct board involvement in high-risk AI decisions
- Combined roles where appropriate (e.g., one person handling both risk and compliance)
- Streamlined documentation processes
- Clear escalation paths for issues
- Regular review meetings combining multiple governance functions.

Medium-sized organizations (50-250 employees) require more formal structures while maintaining operational efficiency. Their governance model typically includes:

- A dedicated AI compliance function, possibly combined with data protection
- Regular management committee meetings on AI governance
- Formal processes for risk assessment and system approval
- Documented policies and procedures for AI development
- Clear separation between development and oversight functions
- Periodic independent reviews of governance effectiveness.

Large Organizations (250+ employees): Large organizations require comprehensive governance structures that can effectively manage multiple AI systems across various business units. Their model should incorporate:

- Board-level AI oversight committee
- Dedicated AI ethics and compliance team
- Specialized roles for risk assessment and quality assurance
- Formal policies and procedures covering all aspects of AI development
- Regular internal audits of compliance

- Comprehensive training programs
- Integration with enterprise risk management systems.

Regardless of size, all organizations must ensure their governance model addresses three fundamental aspects:

- **Decision Authority**. Clear processes for approving AI deployments, with appropriate checks and balances in place based on the risk level. High-risk systems require more rigorous approval processes, which may involve external expertise.

- **Risk Management**. Systematic approaches to identifying and mitigating AI-related risks are tailored to the organization's capabilities, while also meeting regulatory requirements.

- **Oversight Mechanisms**. Regular monitoring and review of AI systems, with frequency and depth determined by risk level and organizational capacity.

The governance model should evolve as the organization grows or its AI usage expands. Regular reviews should assess whether the current model remains appropriate for the organization's size and risk profile.

5.2.2 Role allocation and responsibility matrices

Who's responsible when an AI system makes a questionable decision? The AI Act sets clear obligations, but organizations need thoughtful internal role assignments. At the center stands the AI Compliance Officer, who harmonizes technical requirements with regulatory demands, serving as both internal coordinator and primary contact with supervisory authorities.

Technical leaders strike a balance between innovation and compliance, while risk management teams develop frameworks for evaluating AI-specific risks, which are particularly crucial for high-risk systems. Quality assurance teams verify regulatory compliance, documentation completeness, and human oversight mechanisms.

Organizations should develop detailed responsibility matrices for key AI processes, explicitly defining who is responsible for deployment decisions, control implementation, performance monitoring, incident management, and authority communication. Consider a customer service AI deployment: the Compliance Officer reviews requirements, technical leaders implement controls, risk managers assess impacts, and quality assurance validates both performance and compliance. This clear allocation ensures everyone understands their role while maintaining innovation agility.

5.2.3 Key stakeholder identification and engagement

Who needs to be involved in AI governance? The answer extends far beyond your technical teams. Successful AI compliance requires engaging a diverse ecosystem of stakeholders, each bringing unique perspectives and needs. Let's explore how to build and maintain these crucial relationships.

Your development teams serve as the foundation for implementing AI governance. They transform regulatory requirements into a practical reality through code, testing protocols, and documentation. However, their role extends beyond implementation—they often identify potential issues before they become problems. That's why organizations need to create open channels for developers to raise concerns and contribute to governance improvements. When developers feel heard, they become active partners in building trustworthy AI systems rather than just following rules.

Business units deploying AI systems must understand compliance without being overwhelmed by technical complexity. Their hands-on experience with system deployment and customer interaction provides invaluable insights for refining governance approaches. Think of a sales team using an AI-powered customer prediction tool—their practical feedback helps ensure governance requirements remain realistic and effective.

Senior management requires a different perspective, one that focuses on strategic implications and risk exposure. They require clear metrics that connect AI governance to broader corporate objectives. Board members, in particular, must understand how AI compliance affects organizational strategy and risk management. Regular briefings should translate technical details into business impact, enabling informed decision-making at the highest levels.

Consider how this works in practice: When deploying an AI-powered recruitment system, HR teams provide insight into practical usage, developers ensure technical compliance, senior management oversees risk exposure, and candidates receive clear information about how the system affects their applications. Each stakeholder's perspective contributes to building a more robust and trustworthy system.

5.2.4 Documentation and tracking systems

Think of AI documentation as a living ecosystem rather than a static library. At its foundation lie board-approved policies that establish your governance principles and risk appetite. These documents speak the language of business strategy while maintaining clear connections to regulatory requirements. They set the tone for everything that follows.

From these foundations flow detailed procedures that transform high-level policies into practical workflows. These documents serve as bridges, helping development teams understand how to implement governance requirements in their daily work. They cover crucial processes such as risk assessment, system validation, and incident response, always maintaining a delicate balance between technical precision and practical usability.

At the implementation level, we dive into the technical details—system architecture, data flows, and control mechanisms. While this documentation must be thorough enough for development teams, it shouldn't become impenetrable to compliance functions. The key is demonstrating clear links between technical implementations and regulatory requirements.

However, modern AI governance demands more than static documents. Organizations need digital platforms that bring documentation to life. Real-time compliance monitoring integrates with development pipelines, tracking key performance indicators and maintaining audit trails of system changes. Risk management systems continuously monitor indicators and trigger alerts when needed. Performance analytics track everything from system reliability to the effectiveness of human oversight.

Consider a practical example: When your AI system makes a decision, your documentation platform should automatically record the decision, track its performance, monitor for potential risks, and maintain a clear audit trail—all while ensuring that these records comply with regulatory requirements. This dynamic approach turns documentation from a bureaucratic burden into a valuable tool for system improvement.

5.3 Risk management and compliance systems

How do we adapt traditional risk management to the age of AI? While organizations have spent years developing frameworks for operational, financial, and compliance risks, AI systems present unique challenges that require fresh thinking about risk assessment and management.

5.3.1 Risk assessment methodologies and frameworks

Traditional risk management starts with identifying potential threats and vulnerabilities through expert interviews, historical analysis, and scenario planning. We then evaluate these risks using frameworks ranging from simple likelihood-impact matrices to complex probabilistic models. But AI systems require us to think differently about what constitutes a risk and how we measure it.

Consider the concept of "technical robustness" introduced by the EU AI Act. An AI system isn't simply "safe" or "unsafe"—its reliability exists on a spectrum that can shift over time. We must continuously evaluate how our systems handle errors, adapt to new situations, and maintain performance stability. This means moving beyond point-in-time assessments to implement continuous monitoring and evaluation processes.

Data quality and algorithmic impact present another crucial challenge. When assessing the risks of an AI system, we must consider potential biases, fairness implications, and potential performance degradation over time. This requires breaking down silos between technical teams and risk management functions. A credit scoring algorithm, for example, might show excellent technical performance while harboring subtle biases that create business and compliance risks.

Human oversight emerges as a distinct risk dimension under the AI Act. It's not enough to have theoretical control mechanisms—we must evaluate their practical effectiveness. Can operators truly understand system outputs? Do they have the training and tools to intervene effectively? These questions bridge technical system design with operational reality.

Documentation (see Section 5.1.3 above) plays a crucial role in this enhanced risk framework. We must maintain records that demonstrate not just what decisions were made but why they were made and how they're being monitored. This documentation serves multiple audiences, from internal oversight teams to regulatory authorities, and must tell a clear story about how we identify and manage AI risks.

5.3.2 Compliance monitoring and verification processes

Consider AI compliance monitoring as operating across three distinct time horizons. We track immediate system behavior in real-time through key performance indicators that may signal compliance drift or emerging risks. Over the medium term, we analyze trends to identify gradual shifts in system behavior that may go unnoticed on a day-to-day basis. Finally, longer-term verification processes provide deeper insights into system performance and regulatory alignment, often bringing in external validation.

The foundation of effective monitoring lies in establishing clear, measurable indicators that map directly to regulatory requirements. Consider human oversight of high-risk systems under the EU AI Act. It's not enough to track how often humans intervene—we need to measure the effectiveness and timeliness of these interventions. Similarly, when the Act requires system accuracy and reliability, we must define specific performance thresholds and continuously monitor them. This includes logging, both for regulatory compliance purposes and to help understand system behavior and identify potential issues before they become problems.

When monitoring reveals potential issues, clear escalation pathways become crucial. Organizations need well-defined processes for investigation, intervention, and remediation. Consider a customer service AI that begins to exhibit subtle bias in its responses—the monitoring system should promptly flag this trend, trigger appropriate reviews, and document both the issue and the response.

5.3.3 Incident response and reporting procedures

AI incidents present unique challenges in detection, analysis, and regulatory reporting, often manifesting as "silent failures" where systems maintain apparent functionality while exhibiting subtle issues, such as bias or degraded decision quality. Organizations must bridge technical and regulatory perspectives in their response procedures.

The EU AI Act requires reporting incidents affecting fundamental rights, safety, or legal interests to supervisory authorities. Organizations must translate these regulatory thresholds into observable technical indicators by implementing automated monitoring systems that track key metrics, such as prediction accuracy and decision consistency. Statistical process control methodologies help establish normal operating boundaries and trigger alerts for deviations.

Response procedures should include clear decision trees for incident classification and escalation, guiding teams through assessment protocols that evaluate both the technical severity and regulatory significance of incidents. For example, while accuracy drops might trigger only a technical investigation, behavioral bias affecting protected characteristics would activate both a technical response and compliance reporting.

Organizations should implement incident management platforms that integrate monitoring alerts, response workflows, and communication systems. These platforms must support efficient collaboration among technical teams, compliance officers, and management, while maintaining appropriate access controls and documentation to ensure regulatory compliance.

5.4 Human oversight and control mechanisms

How can we design oversight mechanisms that strike a balance between human judgment and AI efficiency? Human oversight plays a crucial role in ensuring that AI systems operate safely and ethically, particularly as new regulations, such as the EU AI Act, come into effect. Just as an air traffic controller monitors multiple aircraft to ensure safety, organizations need well-designed systems for humans to effectively supervise AI.

5.4.1 Defining oversight roles and responsibilities

When setting up human oversight for AI, organizations need to establish a three-layered structure that functions like a well-oiled machine. Think of it as a building with different floors, each serving a crucial purpose in ensuring AI systems are safe and compliant with regulations, such as the EU AI Act.

On the top floor, we have strategic oversight, where the board and executives set ground rules. Just as a company's leadership team sets the budget and overall direction, these leaders define how much risk the organization will take with AI and ensure there are enough resources to properly manage these systems.

The middle floor houses our operational oversight team—the daily decision-makers bridging the gap between technical complexities and business needs. These professionals are like air traffic controllers for AI, monitoring systems on a day-to-day basis and ensuring everything runs smoothly while maintaining detailed records of their activities.

On the ground floor, we have technical oversight—the foundation of our building. These experts dive deep into system performance, data quality, and algorithm behavior. They're like mechanics who understand every moving part of the AI engine and can spot potential issues before they become problems.

For this structure to function effectively, we require clear lines of communication and well-defined decision-making authority. Imagine a fire evacuation plan in a building—everyone needs to know exactly what to do and who to contact in different situations. The same applies here: organizations must establish explicit protocols for when and how to intervene with AI systems, as well as who has the authority to make different types of decisions.

We also need to tailor this oversight structure to each organization's unique context. A small startup utilizing AI for customer service will require a different approach than a large bank employing AI for fraud detection. Organizations should consider their size, the complexity of their AI applications, and their available expertise when designing their oversight roles.

Regular check-ups are crucial for maintaining the smooth operation of this system. Just as buildings require regular maintenance inspections, organizations should also regularly review their oversight mechanisms to ensure they are effective and up-to-date with new regulations and technological advancements.

5.4.2 Establishing clear intervention protocols

Creating effective intervention protocols is like designing an emergency response system for AI. We need clear rules for when and how humans should step in. This requires designing protocols across several key dimensions:

- Intervention Spectrum:
    o Routine adjustments (like fine-tuning parameters)
    o Corrective actions (addressing edge cases)
    o Emergency responses (halting operations when critical issues arise)

- Time-sensitivity Considerations:
    o Immediate intervention requirements (AI trading systems making unusual decisions)
    o Short-term evaluation windows (customer-facing AI showing bias)
    o Deliberative review processes (AI-generated content for publication)

- Information Requirements:
    o Critical metrics for decision-making
    o Contextual data for informed judgment
    o Historical patterns for comparative analysis

For these protocols to be effective, operators require clear visibility into what the AI system is doing. Imagine having a car dashboard that not only shows your speed but also helps you understand complex engine performance in simple terms. We need similar tools for AI oversight—displays and alerts that translate complex system behavior into information that humans can quickly understand and act on.

Another key consideration is who has the authority to make different decisions. Just as a hospital has different levels of authority for medical decisions, we need clear chains of command for AI interventions. The technical staff may handle some adjustments, while others may require executive approval. These decision-making structures need to be crystal clear to everyone involved.

These protocols shouldn't exist in isolation; they must fit smoothly into existing workflows. It's like adding safety checks to an assembly line: they need to be effective without halting the entire process.

We achieve this by carefully designing intervention points that align with natural breaks in operational processes.

Training is essential for making these protocols work in practice. Just as pilots spend time in flight simulators, oversight personnel need regular practice with realistic scenarios. This helps them build confidence and competence in handling different situations, from routine adjustments to critical interventions.

Finally, we need to treat these protocols as living documents that improve over time. Regular reviews and updates based on real-world experience help us refine our approach. It's like updating safety procedures after learning from incidents—each experience provides valuable insights for making our oversight more effective.

5.4.3 Training requirements for oversight personnel

Training effective AI oversight personnel is like preparing air traffic controllers—they must master technical systems and safety regulations to make critical decisions. Let's explore how to build a comprehensive training program that equips these professionals with the right mix of skills.

The foundation starts with understanding how AI systems work, much like a pilot needs to understand aircraft mechanics. However, this technical knowledge must be immediately applied to real-world requirements, especially regulations such as the EU AI Act. It's not enough to know how the system operates—oversight personnel need to understand when and why they must take action to remain compliant with the law.

We build on this foundation with layers of specialized knowledge. Think of it as learning to read multiple instruments at once—oversight personnel must learn to monitor system performance, spot potential issues, and know when to intervene. This includes understanding both technical warning signs (such as unusual system behavior) and regulatory triggers (such as when certain checks become legally required).

Risk assessment skills form another crucial part of the training. Just as emergency responders must quickly evaluate complex situations, oversight personnel must assess both technical and legal risks in real-time. They must learn to recognize when a situation requires extra attention, even if the system appears to be running smoothly.

Creating documentation is a critical skill that requires dedicated training. Like medical professionals maintaining patient records, oversight personnel must learn to keep clear, complete records that serve both practical needs and legal requirements. This includes mastering documentation systems and understanding how to create audit trails that demonstrate compliance.

Practical experience is gained through scenario-based training, similar to flight simulators used by pilots. By practicing with realistic situations, from routine monitoring to critical incidents, personnel develop the judgment needed for effective oversight. These exercises help bridge the gap between theoretical knowledge and practical application.

Communication skills tie everything together. Oversight personnel must act as bridges between technical teams and management, translating complex issues into clear actions and decisions. It's like being a translator who needs to speak both the language of technology and the language of business and regulation.

5.4.4 Monitoring the effectiveness of human controls

To ensure that human oversight is effective, we need robust monitoring systems that measure both quantitative and qualitative control effectiveness. Just as we track vital signs in healthcare, we monitor specific indicators of oversight health, like intervention frequency, response times, and outcome improvements.

Key metrics should evaluate both the speed and quality of human decisions. For example, in an AI credit decision system, we track not only review frequency but also whether interventions lead to improved customer outcomes. Beyond speed, we need to evaluate decision quality, assessing if operators demonstrate an understanding of risk management and customer protection principles.

Creating strong feedback loops between operators and system designers is essential, much like how pilot feedback enhances aircraft controls. The tools and interfaces our oversight team uses deserve special attention—clunky or confusing interfaces can hinder effective control. Regular evaluation ensures that oversight personnel can effectively interact with systems.

Learning from both successes and failures drives improvement. When incidents occur, we analyze them like accident investigators—not to assign blame, but to understand what helped or hindered effective oversight. Did training prepare operators adequately? Were the protocols clear? These insights help us continuously improve our oversight systems through better training, clearer procedures, and more effective tools.

5.5 Performance monitoring and quality assurance

As AI systems become increasingly integrated into high-stakes decision-making processes, organizations must develop robust mechanisms to continuously assess system performance against both technical specifications and legal obligations.

5.5.1 Introducing monitoring

When we move AI systems from development into real-world operation, we need to transform theoretical safety plans into practical monitoring systems. Building on the risk management principles we explored in Section 5.3, this monitoring goes beyond simple technical checks—it's about ensuring both safety and regulatory compliance. Think of it as moving from testing a new aircraft design to monitoring its flights with passengers aboard.

We begin by establishing meaningful indicators that not only tell us if the system is running, but also if it's making informed decisions. Unlike traditional software, which often focuses mainly on speed and efficiency, AI systems require more sophisticated measurements. These indicators must align with the risk assessment frameworks discussed in Section 5.3, creating clear links between what we're watching and the identified risks. Here's how we structure this monitoring across different timeframes:

Monitoring Dimension	Technical Metrics	Safety Indicators	Compliance Evidence
Immediate Operation	Response accuracy, Processing time, Resource utilization	Decision consistency, Control boundaries, Intervention triggers	Real-time logs, Override records
Medium-term Trends	Performance drift, Data quality metrics, Model stability	Behavioral patterns, Risk indicators, Human oversight effectiveness	Periodic assessments, Incident reports
Long-term Analysis	System evolution, Environmental adaptation, Technical debt	Safety margin trends, Cumulative risk exposure	Audit trails, Compliance documentation

Testing AI systems requires a more comprehensive approach than traditional software validation. We need sophisticated frameworks that evaluate both technical performance and safety implications, connecting back to the oversight mechanisms we covered in Section 5.4. It's like testing not just if an autopilot system works, but ensuring it makes safe decisions across a wide range of scenarios.

Continuous monitoring must catch both immediate issues and subtle patterns that might signal future problems. This system should seamlessly integrate with the incident response procedures outlined in Section 5.3.3. Here's how we structure our monitoring and response framework:

System Aspect	Early Indicators	Response Triggers	Escalation Criteria
Technical Performance	Accuracy deviation, Processing anomalies	Threshold violations, Pattern disruption	Critical degradation, System instability
Safety Measures	Control effectiveness, Decision bounds	Safety margin breach, Oversight gaps	Risk threshold excess, Control failure
Compliance Status	Documentation gaps, Control weaknesses	Regulatory violations, Reporting delays	Material breaches, Systematic issues

5.5.2 On behavioral documentation

Recording and documenting AI behavior is like creating a detailed flight log that captures not just where the plane went, but how it handled different conditions along the way. Building on the governance structures we explored in Section 5.2, we need documentation systems that serve both day-to-day operations and regulatory requirements. This documentation becomes especially valuable when investigating incidents, much like how black box recordings help us understand what happened during a flight.

The core challenge lies in translating AI decisions into records that humans can meaningfully interpret. Drawing from the monitoring frameworks we discussed earlier, we need logging systems that capture three key elements: what decision was made, the situation surrounding that decision, and the key factors that influenced it. This detailed context becomes crucial when connecting with the human oversight mechanisms we covered in Section 5.4—it's like having a clear record of when and why a pilot took control from autopilot.

Time adds another crucial dimension to our documentation needs. Just as subtle changes in engine performance might signal developing issues in an aircraft, AI systems can show gradual behavioral shifts that only become apparent over time. Our documentation systems need to handle both detailed recording of immediate actions and sophisticated tracking of long-term patterns.

5.5.3 Documentation of system behavior

Documenting AI system behavior is more complex than traditional software documentation—it's like trying to record what a student learned and how their learning process evolved over time. While standard version control tracks code changes, we need systems that capture how AI behavior shifts and adapts. This involves recording model updates, tracking changes to the decision boundary, and documenting how the system's responses evolve. We need both automated tracking systems and ways for technical teams and oversight personnel to add their observations and insights.

Connecting system behavior to regulatory compliance presents its own unique challenges. It's not enough to say, "We believe our system complies." We require concrete evidence demonstrating how specific behaviors comply with regulatory requirements. This documentation becomes particularly crucial when dealing with incidents, as discussed in Section 5.3.3. Just as aircraft incident investigations rely on detailed flight records, our behavioral documentation provides essential context for understanding and addressing issues with AI systems.

Looking ahead, we need documentation systems that can grow and adapt as both regulations and technology evolve, like a scientific lab notebook that can accommodate new types of experiments and measurements. Our documentation frameworks must be flexible enough to incorporate new behavioral metrics, enhanced analysis capabilities, and expanded reporting requirements, all while maintaining that crucial bridge between technical operations and regulatory compliance.

5.6 Legal and ethical compliance

The responsible deployment of AI systems requires more than just technical expertise; it is similar to the way practicing medicine demands both scientific knowledge and ethical judgment. While previous sections have explored the practical aspects of keeping AI systems safe through risk management and monitoring, the true mark of a mature organization lies in how seamlessly it weaves legal compliance and ethical considerations into its daily operations.

5.6.1 Beyond compliance: establishing ethical AI frameworks

Moving from basic compliance to truly ethical AI is akin to evolving from following traffic laws to becoming a genuinely responsible driver who considers the safety of everyone on the road. While traditional compliance frameworks give us important rules and checkpoints, they're just the starting point for ethical AI development. Organizations need to stop seeing ethics as just another box to check and instead make it as fundamental to their operations as code quality or system performance.

Ethical AI reaches beyond what regulations explicitly require. Think of it as the difference between what's legally required to sell a car and what makes a car truly safe and beneficial for society. Organizations need sophisticated frameworks that consider these broader impacts while still maintaining rigorous documentation and controls. It's about asking not just "Can we build this?" but "Should we build this?" and "How might this affect different communities?"

Making ethical AI work in practice requires carefully reshaping how organizations operate. Technical teams should feel as comfortable raising ethical concerns as they do reporting technical bugs. Meanwhile, compliance officers require sufficient technical knowledge to understand how design decisions may impact people's lives. This means creating new kinds of collaboration— imagine regular roundtable discussions where engineers, lawyers, and ethicists work together to evaluate new features through multiple lenses.

System design is where ethical frameworks meet real-world implementation. Building on the risk management approaches covered in Section 5.3, organizations need to review their processes to consider both ethical implications and technical specifications. It's like having an environmental impact assessment for construction projects—we need documented evidence showing we've thought through the ethical implications of our technical choices.

Looking ahead, our ethical frameworks must be flexible enough to evolve in tandem with both technological advancements and societal expectations. Just as safety standards for vehicles have evolved in response to new technology and growing awareness of environmental impacts, AI ethics frameworks must adapt while remaining true to their core principles. The goal isn't just to meet today's standards but to build governance systems that can evolve alongside our understanding of AI's impact on society.

5.6.2 Regulatory reporting and accountability structures

Reporting on AI systems to regulators is more complex than traditional compliance reporting—it's akin to providing a comprehensive health report that captures not only current vital signs but also how a patient's condition evolves over time. While conventional compliance may focus on regular checkups with standard metrics, AI systems require more sophisticated reporting that displays both their day-to-day operations and long-term behavioral patterns. This reflects the unique challenges of AI—systems that learn, adapt, and evolve in ways that traditional software doesn't.

The technical challenge lies in translating complex AI behavior into clear, concise compliance stories that regulators can easily understand. Think of it like a doctor explaining complex medical conditions to both patients and insurance companies—we need to be technically accurate while making the information accessible and relevant to regulatory requirements, such as the EU AI Act. Our reporting systems must be able to handle both routine updates and in-depth investigations when regulators have specific questions.

Creating clear accountability for this reporting is crucial. Organizations need well-defined responsibility chains that connect the technical teams monitoring AI systems with the people communicating with regulators. This often means creating specialized roles—think of them as technical translators who understand both AI operations and regulatory requirements. Building on our earlier governance frameworks, these structures establish clear pathways for escalating technical issues to regulatory attention when necessary.

Timing adds another layer of complexity to AI reporting. Unlike traditional compliance, which relies on fixed schedules, AI systems require more flexible reporting approaches. It's like having both regular health checkups and the ability to quickly report emergency conditions. We need protocols that satisfy routine regulatory requirements while allowing us to quickly alert regulators about significant issues.

The real power of regulatory reporting comes from integrating it with broader organizational governance. Our reporting systems should function like a well-designed medical record system, providing management with insights for informed decision-making while offering regulators evidence of proper oversight. This integration helps ensure that our reporting meets both internal needs and external compliance requirements, providing a comprehensive view of how we govern our AI systems.

5.6.3 External validation and certification

External validation for AI systems has evolved far beyond traditional software certification—it's akin to transitioning from basic vehicle safety inspections to comprehensive testing that ensures both technical performance and regulatory compliance. A key driver of this evolution is the emergence of international standards, particularly ISO/IEC frameworks that encompass everything from managing AI throughout its lifecycle to assessing risks and ensuring quality.

The European Union has taken this a step further, making standards conformity the primary means of proving regulatory compliance. This creates a clear business imperative for organizations developing high-risk AI systems: if your system doesn't meet these harmonized standards, organizations won't be able to deploy it. It's like having a CE mark for AI—without it, you can't enter the market.

Implementing certification processes requires meticulous attention to both technical documentation and procedural compliance. Think of it like maintaining aircraft certification records—organizations need comprehensive evidence showing they've followed applicable standards, creating clear audit trails that connect technical choices to specific regulatory requirements. This documentation should flow naturally from the frameworks we discussed earlier, creating a coherent body of evidence that supports both day-to-day operations and regulatory needs.

External validation goes beyond formal certification to include broader stakeholder assurance. Organizations need sophisticated frameworks for working with external auditors, regulators, and independent assessors. It's like hosting safety inspectors in a nuclear power plant—you need to be transparent while protecting sensitive operational details. These frameworks should handle both routine assessments and deeper investigations when issues arise.

The real value of external validation emerges when it's integrated adequately with broader organizational governance. Certification shouldn't just be about getting a stamp of approval—it should drive genuine improvements in how we govern AI systems. This integration helps ensure that external validation serves both immediate compliance needs and long-term organizational goals, creating sustainable frameworks for demonstrating regulatory conformity while advancing AI governance practices.

5.7 Key takeaways

- **Regulatory Frameworks Have Global Impact**: The EU AI Act represents a landmark approach to comprehensive AI regulation, establishing a three-tiered risk-based framework (prohibited practices, high-risk systems, and general AI applications). This approach is gaining global influence, with countries such as Brazil and Korea adopting similar frameworks, while others observe the EU's experience.

- **Governance Requires Layered Implementation**: Effective AI governance demands a three-layered approach that connects boardroom decisions to the actions of the development team. The strategic level establishes policies and risk tolerance, the management layer integrates compliance into existing structures, and the operational level equips development teams with practical tools that maintain innovation agility.

- **Documentation Serves Multiple Purposes**: Documentation under the AI Act isn't merely bureaucratic paperwork but a living record of an AI system's journey that protects organizations, demonstrates compliance, and improves systems. Key components include technical records, risk management trails, and human oversight documentation, all of which require continuous updating as systems evolve.

- **Organizational Implementation Must Scale**: Governance models should reflect organizational reality—from streamlined approaches for small organizations to comprehensive structures for large enterprises, while always addressing three fundamentals: decision authority, risk management, and oversight mechanisms.

- **Human Oversight Requires Structured Design**: Effective human oversight functions like a well-designed building with distinct yet interconnected floors—strategic oversight (board and executives setting ground rules), operational oversight (daily decision-makers bridging technical complexities and business needs), and technical oversight (experts monitoring system performance and algorithm behavior).

- **Performance Monitoring Spans Multiple Timeframes**: AI monitoring must cover immediate operations (response accuracy, decision consistency), medium-term trends (performance drift, human oversight effectiveness), and long-term analysis (system evolution, cumulative risk exposure)—creating a comprehensive framework that connects technical performance with safety and compliance requirements.

- **Ethical AI Requires Going Beyond Compliance**: Moving from basic regulatory adherence to truly ethical AI demands frameworks that consider broader impacts on society and different communities. This requires reshaping organizational culture so that technical teams feel comfortable raising ethical concerns and compliance officers understand the technical implications of design decisions.

- **External Validation Creates Trust**: The EU's approach prioritizes standards conformity as the primary method for demonstrating regulatory compliance. For organizations developing high-risk AI systems, conformity with harmonized standards becomes not just a best practice but a market entry requirement, creating clear business imperatives for robust governance.

CHAPTER 6

AI Safety Education and Awareness

6.0 Introduction

Education and awareness in AI safety matters are equally important to all the design, testing, and legislation work we have discussed for tackling the many risks of AI. This isn't as simple as creating a website, giving a seminar, or even writing a book on the topic. These may all help in some way, but for things to change and AI to become safer, we all need to be aware of this technology and demand that it be improved. After all, all the crucial advances in evolving technology don't start at some university lab, but at people's expectations of them and the growing demand for them in the marketplace. That's why all the topics we discussed in Chapter 1 are relevant, as they are the pain points of this technology that we all need to recognize and become aware of, in order to address them.

Although this topic is vast and next to impossible to cover adequately in a single chapter, we'll attempt to describe its main facets and explore how AI can become safer through specific strategies that an organization or society can apply. Specifically, we'll discuss raising awareness of AI safety concerns, developing educational programs on this topic, promoting AI safety literacy, fostering interdisciplinary collaboration, and refining AI safety standards and guidelines (building upon the existing ones outlined in Chapter 2). At the end of the chapter, we'll also look at a simple exercise to help you start thinking about this topic more and cultivate intuition around it.

6.1 Raising awareness for AI safety concerns

Raising awareness of AI safety concerns is the first step in this initiative. However, it's not that simple if you want to be effective. You could talk to some people at a networking event and that may make them more aware of the whole issue, but would that be enough? Can you rely solely on this in the future? Or will they just forget about it as soon as they leave that event? For awareness-raising to be effective, it needs to be done systematically and in some depth. Here we'll examine three main strategies:

- Highlighting the importance of AI safety in various contexts (domains)
- Explaining the concepts and implications of AI safety, including fairness, transparency, accountability, and robustness
- Encouraging responsible AI development and deployment practices (within a given organization, to start with).

Highlighting the importance of AI safety in various contexts, such as healthcare, finance, and transportation, is a good starting point for our awareness-raising efforts. Places like these may not have the most tech-savvy people, but they may be knowledgeable enough to appreciate the value of safer AI technology. It would make for a more convincing argument than discussing AI safety in general by clarifying the risks of AI in each of these specific contexts. In healthcare, for example, we can highlight that AI may be able to diagnose a terminal condition early on. Still, we may have no idea how it reaches this conclusion or how reliable it is for each individual diagnosis. This could lead to unnecessary psychological turmoil in the patients or worse. Additionally, if the AI system isn't regularly updated, it may miss more and more predictions over time (also known as model drift), all while appearing confident about them. By following AI safety principles and guidelines, we can prevent these issues and ensure that AI is a useful tool, making things easier for all healthcare professionals involved. This awareness-raising tactic can be implemented in specialized seminars or mini-courses, educating both medical professionals and administrators of the corresponding facilities about the importance of this matter. Often, AI-related issues aren't just technical but also people-related, due to stakeholders' limited awareness of such matters.

The next logical step is to explain the concepts and implications of AI safety, including fairness, transparency, accountability, and robustness. This can happen in the same seminars or mini-courses mentioned previously, as people both appreciate and need to hear about solutions for the problems discussed. The biggest challenge here would be to make this knowledge more accessible since these aren't technical people. Using various examples of how a safe AI system exhibits these characteristics in practice, ideally through real-world situations, would be key. Additionally, we can engage in interactive processes to learn more about these matters in depth (see the next section). If even one person in every team becomes more aware of the aspects of AI safety and is capable of discussing them with their colleagues, that would be enough for this initiative, at least.

Encouraging responsible AI development and deployment practices, starting within your organization, is a more practical approach to making AI safe again (this could serve as a motto for the entire initiative!). After all, the only way to have a sustainable impact on a particular sector is by ensuring that individual organizations within that sector adopt this new mindset. People tend to follow those they can trust, and what better way to leverage that than by creating thought leaders in each domain through a few organizations that are ready to make this shift? Data-driven companies are the best place to start, especially if they have already been utilizing AI technology in their workflows. Specific AI development and deployment practices are covered in Chapter 4, although they may need to be adapted to each organization. Generic guidelines may cover the needs of a larger audience, but they can be more challenging to implement. Making these guidelines more specific (as in the case of the exercises in this book, even if the use cases are fictitious) can help make this knowledge more applicable and gradually turn it into know-how.

In parallel, we can also have a specialized AI system for this purpose, designed by an NPO or other organization with AI safety as part of its mission statement. This can be a useful add-on to help keep this knowledge alive and easily accessible, be it through a piece of software on each organization's servers, an app on the employees' mobile devices, or even an API for the organization's engineers to use for making the whole matter of AI safety more interactive and even enjoyable to all the members of the organization (e.g., through internal websites).

6.2 Developing AI safety education programs

Another strategy for educating people on AI safety and raising awareness of the subject is through specialized education programs. This requires special attention, as it's easy to develop something overly generic that may not benefit anyone in particular. Many videos online discuss AI safety in this manner, aiming to appeal to the widest possible audience. Although they succeed in raising some awareness on the matter, whether they do a good job at educating those people is debatable. One promising strategy in this matter involves a combination of action items, including developing curricula for AI ethics, safety, and governance, offering training sessions for developers, users, and policymakers on AI safety considerations, and encouraging interdisciplinary collaboration among AI experts, ethicists, and policymakers. Let's delve into them more.

Developing curricula for AI ethics, safety, and governance is a natural and crucial first step. All of these areas are interconnected, and it's challenging to understand AI safety without also considering the others. AI governance, in particular, is crucial for organizing and conducting an AI project, ensuring it complies with relevant regulations and that the necessary data flows are in place. Even if it doesn't focus on handling the AI risks per se, it provides the infrastructure for making AI safety possible. Naturally, the curricula for these subjects need to be created with the target audience in mind, making it clear that they are intended for them. Many people who are not versed in technical topics may glance at these subjects and decide that they are not relevant to them, but if these curricula are designed to bridge the gap between them and these subjects, they may still be of value. Just as computer technology was highly technical when PCs first emerged, AI safety today faces a similar situation. However, unlike PCs, which didn't have large-scale risks attached to them, AI is a serious matter that needs to be handled carefully, as many of its risks are subtle and difficult to identify. This can serve as a good starting point when developing curricula around these subjects.

Offering training sessions for developers, users, and policymakers on AI safety considerations is another good tactic for developing educational programs. Sometimes, we just need to start small, with a training session or two for specific groups of people involved in AI work. These individuals may already be familiar with this technology, making these training sessions more effective. Policymakers, in particular, may require extensive training on this subject, as they often come from diverse backgrounds that have little to do with technology. And if some of them possess technical expertise (at least on paper), this may not be relevant to AI technology, as many things have changed since then. Once these training sessions gain popularity, we can build larger initiatives around them, including AI safety courses, seminars, etc., that run throughout the year, making more people aware of this subject and how it relates to their everyday lives.

Encouraging interdisciplinary collaboration between AI experts, ethicists, and policymakers is another key vertical of educational initiatives in the AI safety field. The Cosmos Institute has taken this matter seriously and developed an educational process that aims to introduce a more philosophical perspective to this complex and technical issue. The Future of Life Institute has adopted a similar approach, focusing more on mitigating the large-scale risks associated with this technology. In any case, great things can happen when people from different fields collaborate. The more diverse this group is in terms of specializations, the better the outcome is bound to be. We'll talk more about this matter later in the chapter.

6.3 Promoting AI safety literacy

AI safety literacy can be viewed as a specialized kind of data literacy. After all, there is no AI without data. If you are comfortable with the various concepts and processes around data work, chances are that AI safety would come naturally to you. The two are intimately connected and it's hard to advance in one without progressing on the other. As a result, promoting AI safety literacy is likely to enhance one's education on AI- and data-related topics and raise awareness about specific aspects of AI. On a practical level, being familiar with all this and making this knowledge your own would enable you to handle sensitive data more effectively, particularly when dealing with AI systems. You may opt for more reliable systems instead of the off-the-shelf ones that are "free," as they generate revenue from the data they collect from their users. Additionally, you can familiarize yourself with specific protocols that help keep AI interactions safer. AI safety literacy can also help you cultivate a good sense of discernment whereby you can decide intelligently when and how to use an AI system, instead of making it your daily driver out of peer pressure.

In this section, we'll look into some useful tactics related to AI safety literacy. Examples include developing AI safety guides, checklists, and risk assessments for various industries and applications, creating online platforms for sharing best practices, case studies, and lessons learned on AI safety, and promoting peer-to-peer learning and knowledge sharing within the AI community. Naturally, these are just scratching the surface of what's possible, as AI safety literacy, like data literacy in general, is a vast topic that lends itself to a continuous learning schema. For now, we can examine these three key aspects.

Developing AI safety guides, checklists, and risk assessments for various industries and applications is a worthy strategy for promoting AI safety literacy in the real world. After all, sometimes things need to happen systematically for a large enough portion of the population to gain awareness, which may explain why various media outlets are immensely popular nowadays. HACCP has had a similar history, and although it originated primarily in government organizations, such as NASA and the US Army, it eventually reached a broader audience through the Pillsbury company and several other private sector organizations. Nowadays, it's hard not to be familiar with this system if you are involved in production management, particularly in food-related sectors. Perhaps the AI safety guidelines will evolve into something similar, guiding people through clear, straightforward ways to navigate the various risks of AI and the protocols that can help keep them in check. HACCP hasn't eliminated microbiological issues altogether, but the fact that we don't have to take a big risk every time we get some industrial meal or beverage is a win. AI safety can achieve similar successes if we learn from this example and apply it to the AI industry.

Creating online platforms for sharing best practices, case studies, and lessons learned on AI safety can be a powerful supplementary tool in promoting AI safety literacy. This can be something as simple as a Discord server, a series of in-person events and conferences worldwide, or other platforms where people discuss these matters with others, often within their own industry. The principles and guidelines we mentioned in the book's first part may seem abstract and a bit distant from our day-to-day tasks. Still, when we see how others apply them and how it's not as challenging as researching and writing about them, people may start viewing them as something feasible that can add significant value to their daily work routine.

Encouraging peer-to-peer learning and knowledge sharing within the AI community is a similar vertical to the previous one. This one, however, focuses mostly on AI practitioners, including AI researchers, AI developers, AI project managers, and advanced AI users (e.g., data scientists). It's not clear whether prompt engineers would qualify as members of this community, but if the community grows sufficiently, sub-communities may also include such specializations. After all, everyone can be involved in this field, given enough effort, commitment, and know-how, and not everyone needs to contribute the same way. As long as everyone is on the same page regarding AI safety literacy, everyone is likely to benefit from the knowledge transfer that occurs in such communities.

6.4 Fostering interdisciplinary collaboration

Interdisciplinary collaboration is what made the field of AI possible in the first place. So, it makes sense that fostering such collaboration, including a more diverse group of experts, could help stay on top of it, guaranteeing a certain level of AI safety. Ideally, this would be a grassroots movement since top-down initiatives like this rarely have any real-world benefit and end up generating more rules and guardrails than actual solutions to the problems they tackle. A few verticals of this strategy would include items like:

- Establishing AI safety working groups or committees with diverse representation
- Organizing international conferences, workshops, or hackathons on AI safety topics
- Developing partnerships between academia, industry, and government to advance AI safety research and best practices.

Establishing AI safety working groups or committees with diverse representation is one way to foster this interdisciplinary collaboration. This may require a significant amount of administrative overhead, but it may be justified in certain cases. The committees would ideally be created by volunteers from professionals in the groups they represent, and they would need to change periodically to ensure that they don't become career paths for the people involved. Ideally, the individuals in these groups would also continue with their regular duties, even on a part-time basis, to stay connected to the practical aspects of their fields. These teams may also collaborate with AI-related institutes that promote AI safety, such as the ones mentioned previously, to ensure they operate in a well-informed manner. Although there is the risk of them adding a layer of bureaucracy to the whole matter and stifling creativity in AI development, sometimes it may be necessary so that the less responsible players in the AI arena don't make the rules as they go their own way. AI may work well because it optimizes a given fitness function through the advanced algorithms it leverages. However, this fitness function doesn't have to be the profit of a particular multinational company; instead, it should be some KPI that involves everyone on the planet. These AI safety committees may help bring this kind of idea into reality.

Organizing international conferences, workshops, or hackathons on AI safety topics is another effective way to address the issue of AI safety literacy. These can bring together AI developers from various industries, helping them know, learn, and work together on projects they wouldn't otherwise work on. It's extremely challenging to fit an AI safety project into a sprint or a series of sprints when the overarching AI initiative of the organization is focused on achieving a specific business objective. However, if some groundwork has already been laid, it may be easier to introduce such projects in various settings, especially if they are part of a grassroots movement for AI safety. After all, many of the issues this field faces today are due to a lack of communication and/or a lack of mutual understanding. Getting the various players in these fields to communicate with each other and work together would be a good start in mitigating this entire issue.

Developing partnerships among academia, industry, and government to advance AI safety research and best practices is a highly ambitious yet worthy initiative for promoting AI safety literacy. However, there may already be connections among these areas that can serve as a good starting point for developing this network of partnerships. Naturally, this would require an external party to ensure that the aims of these collaborations remain agenda-free, as it's very easy for the interests of one of these entities to spill over into the partnerships and ultimately dominate the entire network. Perhaps involving some non-profits in the mix would help better coordinate the corresponding initiatives and bring about new applied science that benefits everyone in terms of AI safety.

6.5 Developing AI safety standards and guidelines

Developing AI safety standards and guidelines, particularly for specific sectors, is a final strategy for raising awareness and educating the public about this topic. This may seem redundant, as there are already various such standards and guidelines in place, as we saw in the book's first part. However, the fact that they aren't yet well-known to everyone involved in AI is a sign that they may require further refinement. After all, having them on paper is one thing, but promoting them is a completely different matter. Let's examine this strategy in more detail and explore how we can make these abstract concepts more applicable and bring them to life in the context of new AI projects. Namely, let's zero in on specific tactics such as:

- Developing AI-specific safety standards and guidelines for various industries and applications
- Providing clear guidance on AI system design, development, testing, and deployment to ensure safety and reliability
- Encouraging industry adoption of AI safety standards and guidelines.

Developing AI-specific safety standards and guidelines for various industries and applications is the next logical step following the existing general guidelines. After all, each industry has its own characteristics, and the use of AI may vary significantly. For example, AI-based recommender systems in the fashion sector may differ significantly from the content-generation-related AIs used by marketing agencies. The same goes for standards. If an AI in the former yields a bad recommendation to a user, it's not as crucial as an AI in the latter that creates a discriminatory or otherwise offensive post to promote a product or a service. Naturally, there are AI systems that are fairly common across industries, such as the chatbots that are all the rage these days. RAG systems also fall into this category. In any case, the use cases of these systems may also vary across different sectors, which may require more specialized guidelines to accompany their production.

Providing clear guidance on AI system design, development, testing, and deployment to ensure safety and reliability is another important matter for this AI safety education and awareness vertical. This doesn't have to be something rigid and overly generic, however. Just as there are processes in place for optimizing the design, development, testing, and deployment of conventional data products, the same can be applied in the AI world. Data products tend to be inherently safer since they don't have the unpredictable nature of AI systems or the vast training sets associated with them. In any case, the AI field can learn a great deal from the analytics world and take these lessons to a new level, adapting them to each specific use case. This guidance can be provided by thought leaders in the AI world, as well as through mentors, instructors, consultants, and others who are invested in your success. As long as you veer from AI evangelists who have only superficial knowledge of the subject, you should be alright.

Encouraging industry adoption of AI safety standards and guidelines is the natural next step and probably the most challenging one. After all, many people may participate in a seminar about these new standards and guidelines and integrate them intellectually. Still, when it comes to putting them into practice, that's a completely different ball game. Fortunately, as in the previous tactic, there may also be people vested in making a success of all this. Many technical lawyers, for instance, specialize in GDPR and AI Act compliance and make it their mission that you don't have to struggle with these matters. The same goes for consultants who make these AI safety standards part of your organization's workflow. The key here, like in other verticals of AI safety education and awareness, is collaboration. Once you have the right people in your network (not necessarily as full-time employees), you can also progress in this area, making AI safety not just a nice idea but an everyday reality in your workplace.

With these strategies, we conclude our discussion on AI safety education and awareness. Moving forward, we'll explore the necessary steps to take when things don't go according to plan and address AI safety challenges in practice. But first, let's shift gears a bit and see how the following brief exercise can help make the material of this chapter more practical for you and hone your sense of discernment on this vital matter.

6.6 Which of the following initiatives can help with AI safety ed and awareness?

Consider each one of the following and say why or why not they are suitable for this purpose.

1. A video about AI safety in general
2. A demo of an AI gone off the rails
3. An RPG with an AI safety theme
4. A long document describing the risks of AI today
5. A course on AI literacy highlighting viable strategies for safer AI
6. A compilation of reports from whistleblowers in AI development companies
7. An interactive video series featuring AI risks and guidelines
8. A series of blog articles tackling the topic from various angles

9. A set of interviews with experts in this field as part of a podcast on this topic

10. An adventure-like video game where the main character explores a world where AI is unsafe and has to deal with issues stemming from it

11. Posters on the streets in the city center urging the citizens to be more aware of AI safety matters, with a URL for a dedicated website

12. A checklist for an organization to ensure that any AI projects it works on meet certain standards and that the right processes are in place

13. A government-driven think-tank for figuring out better AI safety practices

14. An AI safety literacy book to include in a school curriculum

15. An AI governance book or series of in-depth articles on the topic

16. State- or org-sponsored mentoring on AI safety topics

17. Conferences on AI safety targeting a wider audience (not just AI-savvy people)

18. A dedicated website on AI safety matters for non-tech-savvy people

19. Word-of-mouth education starting from more knowledgeable individuals

20. AI safety events on the meetup.com platform.

Beyond these, what other initiatives can you think of to help educate people about AI safety and raise awareness on this matter?

6.7 Key takeaways

- Education and awareness are crucial for AI safety, requiring strategies such as raising awareness of concerns, developing educational programs, promoting literacy, fostering interdisciplinary collaboration, and establishing standards and guidelines to ensure that people demand safer AI technology.

- Effective awareness-raising efforts for AI safety concerns require a systematic approach that involves three main strategies: highlighting the importance of AI safety in various contexts, explaining key concepts and their implications, and promoting responsible AI development and deployment practices within organizations.

- Another strategy for educating people on AI safety and raising awareness is through specialized education programs, which can include developing curricula for AI ethics, safety, and governance, offering training sessions for developers, users, and policymakers, and encouraging interdisciplinary collaboration between AI experts, ethicists, and policymakers to foster a more philosophical approach to this technical matter.

- AI safety literacy can be viewed as a specialized kind of data literacy, and promoting it can help with education on AI- and data-related topics, raise awareness on AI-specific topics, enable individuals to handle sensitive data better, make informed decisions about AI system use, and cultivate discernment.

- Fostering interdisciplinary collaboration between experts from various fields is crucial for promoting AI safety literacy, which can be achieved through strategies such as establishing AI safety working groups or committees with diverse representation, organizing international conferences, workshops, or hackathons on AI safety topics, and developing partnerships between academia, industry, and government to advance AI safety research and best practices.

- Developing AI safety standards and guidelines, especially specific to particular sectors, is a key strategy for raising awareness of AI safety and educating people about it, which can be achieved through tactics such as developing AI-specific safety standards and guidelines for various industries and applications, providing clear guidance on AI system design, development, testing, and deployment to ensure safety and reliability, and encouraging industry adoption of AI safety standards and guidelines.

CHAPTER 7

Addressing AI Safety Challenges

7.0 Introduction

Although pinpointing the areas of AI safety that need improvement and raising awareness on this matter is crucial, all efforts will be for nothing if we remain there. To make an impact in the AI safety field, to the extent our circumstances allow, we need to address the various AI safety challenges we have become aware of and develop constructive collective habits around that. Namely, we can do one or more of the following: confront unintended consequences of AI (ensuring alignment), mitigate adversarial attacks (ensuring better robustness), improve transparency and explainability (getting rid of the black box to some extent, enhancing interpretability), address fairness and non-discrimination (making sure the AI is less biased), develop ethical frameworks (to ensure AI is used in the most ethical way possible), and foster international cooperation on this matter (bringing together experts from various areas). These are summarized in Figure 3 on the next page.

Considering the previous chapters, these points may seem obvious, especially if you've been paying attention. However, how exactly we can apply them is less obvious and particularly important. Additionally, these can be a starting point for new initiatives and solutions to the AI safety problem, so there is plenty of room for creativity on your part to help make AI safer. Even if the solutions you come up with are not definite or applicable on a larger scale, if they can help your team or your organization, that's a good starting point. If everyone did the same, the issue of AI safety would be resolved or at least under control in no time. So, let's get to it and see how we can stay ahead of the curve with AI, keeping it a useful tool rather than a ticking time bomb.

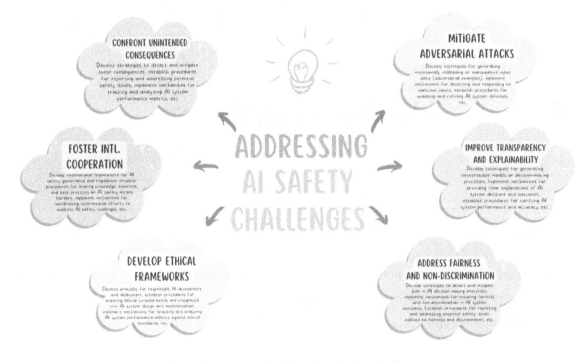

Figure 3: Strategies for addressing AI safety challenges.

7.1 Confront unintended consequences

Let's start this endeavor of addressing AI safety challenges with the most apparent issue of AI: unintended consequences and how to confront them. After all, if we were to handle the situations where AI doesn't behave as intended, we'd be left with the situations where it responds as we expect. Things aren't that simple, however, as there are many situations whereby an AI system can deviate from its expect path of action. So, we'd first need to develop strategies to detect and mitigate these consequences. Then, we'd have to establish procedures for reporting and addressing potential safety issues. Finally, we'll need to implement mechanisms for tracking and analyzing the performance metrics of our AI system. Let's explore these strategies in more detail and examine how they relate to one another.

Developing strategies to detect and mitigate these consequences is a straightforward first step. This can be done by compiling a list of the unintended consequences across different time frames. It's not enough to look only at the short-term, as many AI initiatives tend to do, but also to explore the medium- and long-term consequences. Additionally, it's beneficial to examine the consequences for various users and other stakeholders. It's not enough to tackle the unintended consequences of some response of the AI system, but also look at how subtle issues with the responses may create issues to various people, including those affected by the AI systems indirectly (e.g., people losing their jobs). These subtle issues may require a different perspective to pinpoint and address, as they aren't always obvious. One such scenario is when people become increasingly dependent on AI systems for their everyday lives, often referred to as "life on autocomplete." This may not happen in the near future. Still, the possibility of it occurring is undeniable, especially if we don't acknowledge it as an unintended consequence of widespread use of AI.

Naturally, not all consequences are going to be of the same gravity. That's why we'd need to evaluate the severity of these consequences, perhaps through a panel of experts or individuals with sufficient experience in these matters who have a vested interest. The most diverse this panel is, the better the chances of it being of value in its mission. Of course, its scope may be limited to a particular organization, but that's still a good starting point. If every AI-related organization adopted such an approach to the unintended consequences of its AI systems, the problem wouldn't be as pronounced, and synergies would form organically as everyone would benefit from a collaborative approach to this matter.

Establishing procedures for reporting and addressing potential safety issues is the next logical step after listing and evaluating the unintended consequences. We can start by prioritizing the most challenging problems and incorporating processes into the AI systems to facilitate easier reporting of these issues. Beyond that, it would be beneficial to perform analytics regularly for these issues, e.g., using dashboards that make this information easily accessible to stakeholders. This way, we can be proactive about these issues, tackling them before they escalate or trigger larger problems that may seem unmanageable (e.g., an AI system running amok, people catastrophizing about it, etc.).

Implementing mechanisms for tracking and analyzing AI system performance metrics is another strategy for handling unintended consequences that complements the previous ones. In this case, the metrics for the AI system performance would relate to matters of alignment and mitigation of the unintended consequences. It's not enough for an AI system to be swift or avoid hallucinations; it needs to be able to provide value in the long-term without dropping the ball on the subtle aspects of its role. Involving the aforementioned panel in the development of these tracking and analysis of these metrics is crucial. After all, these are powerful KPIs and need to be treated this way, instead of yet another set of metrics that people will forget as soon as they are calculated. Ideally, these metrics will be factored in every strategic decision of the AI system and have people involved in owning them, ensuring that they are within certain operational parameters.

A more practical way to work towards this would be to have a reinforcement learning module in the AI system based on the feedback of human users. This can be both personalized (for each individual using the system) and general, as certain feedback may be relevant to incorporate for everyone using the system. Naturally, there needs to be a human in the loop overseeing how the patterns of this feedback affect the system, ensuring that the AI system's evolution is well-paced and manageable. Beyond the users, other stakeholders of the system may be able to provide their feedback too, ensuring that the system gets more holistic feedback for its functionality and its alignment with our collective values. This may not always be easy, but it's certainly doable, and with enough work on this vertical, it may even be a standard for all AI systems moving forward.

7.2 Mitigate adversarial attacks

Mitigating adversarial attacks is big, especially considering current AI systems' vulnerabilities, particularly LLMs. Such systems have vulnerabilities that have started to get more widely known, making them easy prey to all kinds of malicious actors who want to abuse them somehow or are after the training data they conceal in their networks. Considering the vast number of possibilities for prompts, figuring out what can be a potentially malicious prompt isn't easy, and, as a result, we need to be methodical about it. In practice, to mitigate adversarial attacks on an AI system, we need to develop techniques for generating intentionally misleading or manipulative input data, implement mechanisms for detecting and responding to malicious inputs, and finally establish procedures for updating and refining AI system defenses. Let's explore each one of these strategies in more depth.

Developing techniques for generating intentionally misleading or manipulative input data, also known as adversarial examples, is a necessary strategy. This can be achieved in various ways, ranging from curated prompts to automatically generated content, such as that which a specialized generative AI can create for this purpose. It's not easy to "break" an AI system this way, especially one of the more modern ones. However, given enough attempts and some creativity, it is possible to uncover vulnerabilities that may cause the system to output its training data or yield responses that compromise its functionality. Beyond these more well-known techniques, a widely used approach in cybersecurity is the bug bounty method. This involves providing monetary rewards to white-hat hackers who discover ways to break a cybersecurity system, thereby unveiling potential bugs within it. This way, the engineers of that system can fix them before other hackers discover and exploit them. Versions of this approach can also be applied to AI safety, with knowledgeable AI users taking similar precautions for AI systems that are vulnerable to specific prompts.

Implementing mechanisms for detecting and responding to malicious inputs is another essential strategy that complements the previous one. After all, knowing about the bugs isn't enough; we need to be able to fix them or manage them until a fix is developed and deployed. This may involve things like identifying a potentially problematic prompt and bypassing the normal response, or even halting the system altogether and initiating a curated response that's created programmatically. This may seem like patching a system, but it's not a bad first step until the issue is properly understood and tackled effectively. Sometimes, retraining the AI system may be required, which can be time-consuming and impractical. For AI systems to be useful, they must be practical first and foremost.

Establishing procedures for updating and refining AI system defenses is a good way to extend the previous strategies, making our whole approach more proactive. This involves developing a virtual armor of sorts for the AI system to protect it from these adversarial attacks before they can affect it in any way. Essentially, it is equivalent to creating a cyber shield that prevents malicious users from abusing it while keeping it useful for its well-intentioned users. There is a fine balance between usability and security, and often a trade-off between them. However, with these procedures and refinements, we can find a suitable balance where the AI system remains useful while also being secure. It's all about optimizing a certain value function. We need to include the cost of the system becoming compromised in this entire equation, rather than just focusing on performance metrics.

Beyond all this, we can also enhance our approach to addressing this AI vulnerability by utilizing a state-of-the-art AI system that monitors other AIs for potential backdoors. Although this is not specifically geared towards adversarial attacks, it can help mitigate various situations where an AI is compromised, either through a malicious prompt or programmatically.

7.3 Improve transparency and explainability

Improving transparency and explainability is a thorny matter, as most AI systems are designed differently. However, if we were to enhance this single aspect of AI, the improvements that would ensue would make the whole technology much better and safer across different verticals. So, no matter how challenging this aspect of AI is, it's worth pursuing and eventually accomplishing. In practice, this would involve developing techniques for generating interpretable models or decision-making processes, implementing mechanisms to provide clear explanations of AI system decisions and outcomes, and establishing procedures for verifying AI system performance and accuracy. Let's look into each one of these points in more detail.

Developing techniques for generating interpretable models or decision-making processes is crucial for improving transparency and explainability, as well as providing an infrastructure. For this to happen, we need to develop either methods for interpreting the operations that take place in the neural networks of these systems or design new ones from scratch that are interpretable. So far, most efforts have been concentrated on the first vertical, which has made the most sense. However, it might be worth exploring the second option as well, as this is likely to be easier to work with than the first version. Decision-making processes may be easier to work with, but this also depends on how much these processes depend on legacy black box systems. Decision science has traditionally employed various models, so it's up to us to opt for the more transparent ones or even develop new ones from scratch with built-in transparency. The cost of these initiatives may seem steep, but in the long run, it may be justified, as it would lead to more robust predictions and decisions that are less likely to take us by surprise or carry biases and errors.

Implementing mechanisms for providing clear explanations of AI system decisions and outcomes is a logical next step for all this. This is likely to involve new modules and processes, as well as new metrics for measuring the clarity of the decisions. Involving a variety of stakeholders and experts in this process would make it easier to gain a holistic view of the new systems and explore how they can be further improved. After all, this is most likely an ongoing process since explainability isn't as simple as an LLM justifying its output; it involves being able to peek at the operations that lead the system to come up with the output in the first place, establishing a measure of confidence, and eventually linking the inputs with the outputs in a clear-cut way. This is particularly useful and challenging in complex decisions that involve numerous calculations and assumptions, which must be made as explicitly as possible.

Establishing procedures for verifying AI system performance and accuracy, particularly in an explainable way, is paramount as a strategy. After all, there is a trade-off between explainability and accuracy in most machine learning systems. Hence, we need to make sure that the added explainability doesn't interfere with the AI system's performance. However, this trade-off isn't inevitable, and advanced predictive analytics systems can be developed that are both accurate and easy to understand (e.g., neuro-fuzzy systems like ANFIS). The issue lies in scalability since additional variables make explainability more challenging. Nevertheless, this issue can often be alleviated with clever dimensionality reduction methods. If these were made to be explainable and transparent, we might be on to something. In any case, adding a layer of explainability to an AI system can help us understand it better and possibly improve it in ways we couldn't otherwise. Instead of the brute-force approach to high performance, we can explore architectures that optimize performance without having a large number of layers or nodes in those layers. All this can help AI systems evolve more intelligently, while keeping us informed about how they operate.

Beyond these approaches, as an interim solution to the black-box issue of AI, we can explore methods like CMA-ES, which have been proven effective in systems such as CLIP and ChatGPT. This enables the systems to "forget" 40% of the classes in a given dataset, making them more adept at recognizing the remaining courses (i.e., the AIs become more specialized), while also creating a layer of security within the data itself (https://bit.ly/3EmXtx0). This approach may not yield a transparent AI system, but it may help mitigate the problems of non-transparent AIs until a better solution comes along.

Additionally, systems like the *Deep Seek R1* AI and *Grok3*, which focus on providing the user with a chain of thought (also known as inner dialogue) behind their answers, are a step in the right direction. These kinds of systems are especially useful in problem-solving tasks and complex decision-making, where transparency is more useful, if not essential.

7.4 Address fairness and non-discrimination

This vertical of AI safety is closely linked to the changing societal norms and values that an AI system must adapt to over time. It involves numerous subtle matters that may be difficult to gauge at first, but which are crucial to the individuals directly involved and to society as a whole. To manage this challenge, we need to look into each one of the following verticals:

- Develop strategies to detect and mitigate bias in AI decision-making processes
- Implement mechanisms for ensuring fairness and non-discrimination in AI system outcomes
- Establish procedures for reporting and addressing potential safety issues related to fairness and discrimination.

Developing strategies to detect and mitigate bias in AI decision-making processes is crucial in this area. We can first carefully assess the bias of each output or decision the AI system yields, ideally measuring it with specialized metrics. This may be a time-consuming process, as it's not always easy to determine the bias of a statement before scrutinizing it. AI systems tend to be very convincing about their objectivity, even when they lack it. However, over time, we may be able to develop a heuristic check for bias and apply it to gauge the AI system in this respect. The measure may not be 100% accurate, but it may still be useful, like most heuristics. If this approach is coupled with efforts to make the system more transparent, we may be able to pinpoint specific data points that cause the biases and retrain the system after adjusting the training set accordingly.

Implementing mechanisms to ensure fairness and non-discrimination in AI system outcomes is a prudent follow-up strategy. After all, detecting biases is one thing, but if we don't do something to mitigate them, that's not really a value-add. Naturally, we need to have safeguards in place so that when an AI system yields an output that's unfair or has discriminatory elements, users should be able to report it. This can also help adjust the bias metrics, making them more accurate. Of course, not all feedback from the users needs to be treated the same, since some users may be more sensitive than others on such matters. Finding a good balance between constructive feedback and UX design may not be easy, but it's feasible over time. How we handle user feedback may depend on various factors, and with the right processes in place, we can maximize its benefits without making drastic changes to the AI from one day to the next. Ideally, the majority of the system's core users should be satisfied with its lack of biases, even if they still identify points of potential improvement. Keeping the points of serious concern at bay may be sufficient, as we don't want to overfit the AI system on this matter, thereby jeopardizing its overall usefulness.

Establishing procedures for reporting and addressing potential safety issues related to fairness and discrimination is a necessary complementary strategy. This ties in closely with the previous strategy, although it may be addressed differently. For example, the option to report a safety concern about the AI system may be implemented more responsibly to prevent users from abusing it. Some individuals are overly sensitive to this matter and may never be satisfied with the changes the AI team makes to the system. Therefore, it's essential to distinguish between the feedback and reporting functions, with the latter being more comprehensive and detailed. For serious safety issues, the user may be asked to provide specific examples with screenshots to illustrate the concerns raised. For feedback, on the other hand, a simple rating of the output over a couple of factors may be sufficient. Naturally, it would be beneficial to have individuals specializing in this area within the organization, or across different organizations, who can evaluate and quantify issues related to fairness and discrimination. These individuals may even interact with the users who raise concerns and attempt to identify the underlying issues, liaise with AI engineers, and develop potential solutions to the problems.

A key issue related to AI safety is the changing societal norms and values that an AI system needs to navigate intelligently. After all, society isn't static, so our modes of life and values change as we change. Rather than being rigid about all this, an AI system needs to understand that and adapt accordingly. This can be achieved through both regular system retraining using up-to-date data on these matters and leveraging user feedback and engagement metrics. Perhaps the AI system can take into account how user behavior changes over time for various societal topics and extract patterns around this. Care must be taken, however, so that these changes aren't too drastic, as the AI system needs to maintain a sense of stability. Otherwise, it may be prone to manipulation.

7.5 Develop ethical frameworks

Ethical frameworks may seem unnecessary to those leading an AI development project, especially when there is a strict deadline to meet. However, even if the ethics of AI don't yield value-added benefits that directly affect the bottom line, they are still important and help prevent bigger issues that arise if this aspect of AI isn't addressed adequately. To achieve this, we need to develop principles for responsible AI development and deployment, establish procedures to ensure that ethical considerations are integrated into AI system design and implementation, and implement mechanisms for tracking and analyzing AI system performance metrics against established ethical standards. This needs to happen both at a high level and at a lower level, too, making this entire strategy a practice that everyone involved in AI projects can easily understand and follow.

Developing principles for responsible AI development and deployment may seem daunting, but it's an essential first step. Even if some organizations have taken this step through the development of guidelines, we discussed in the first part of the book, these need to be made more applicable to each organization. We need to first define what ethical AI means to us, along with any follow-up questions that may arise. For example, how does having a more ethical AI system translate into specific behaviors, functionalities, and user experiences (UX)? Additionally, how will this ethical aspect of AI improve the overall situation in ways that make it more desirable? After all, if we don't have a strong motivation for making all these changes, it would be difficult to sustain them. Just as there are several search engines geared towards privacy, which have this as a key characteristic to attract more users and make them their go-to place for accessing the web, the same could happen with AI systems that are geared towards being more ethical.

A necessary supporting strategy is to establish procedures for ensuring ethical considerations are integrated into AI system design and implementation. These ethical AI initiatives need to be made concrete, with specific processes integrated into the development and maintenance workflows. AI systems need to be rethought so that they are developed with total quality principles in mind, opting for continuous improvement in these areas. This will translate into new sets of KPIs that would be factored in heavily in the newer versions of the AI systems, putting robustness and reliability at the forefront of these systems. Values alignment will need to be considered constantly when developing a new iteration of the AI, rather than being an afterthought or something briefly mentioned at the beginning and then forgotten.

Implementing mechanisms for tracking and analyzing AI system performance metrics against ethical standards is a powerful step for ensuring that the ethical consideration is a continuous process that's managed properly over time. The aforementioned KPIs can be a good starting point for that. Additionally, specialized committees may be involved in all this, ideally not directly related to the specific branch, to maintain objectivity. These can guide the overall process and ensure that it is conducted in accordance with the originally agreed-upon ethical frameworks.

7.6 Foster international cooperation

Many organizations have already begun fostering international cooperation to address various issues related to AI safety, such as the Future of Life Institute. However, to succeed in this ambitious mission, they would need the support of everyone. It's possible that additional initiatives would need to be launched or expanded to include more organizations. In brief, this vertical of AI safety encompasses developing international frameworks for AI safety governance and regulation, establishing procedures for sharing knowledge, expertise, and best practices on AI safety across borders, and implementing mechanisms for coordinating international efforts to address AI safety challenges. Let's explore each one of them one by one.

Developing international frameworks for AI safety governance and regulation is a necessary step in fostering international cooperation on this matter. Although this can occur in various ways, it is best to start from a place of awareness rather than relying solely on regulations. Through a robust educational framework that raises everyone's data literacy level, with a focus on AI, for example, stakeholders of AI projects can become more appreciative of the importance of proper data governance, as well as the governance of the corresponding AI technologies. This may not be easy, but it's certainly feasible and value-adding in the long-term. After all, most significant developments in the AI field have occurred because people from diverse backgrounds have come together across borders to advance this technology. Would it be far-fetched to think that this is the best way to continue progressing in this field?

Establishing procedures for sharing knowledge, expertise, and best practices on AI safety across borders is the next logical step. This can be specialized conferences (particularly application-oriented), seminars, workshops, and even competitions for designing and building the safest AI system. Additionally, we can establish specialized forums where everyone can share their experiences and seek out mentors on this subject. Naturally, we can also continue to have journals and other publications, augmenting the existing body of knowledge and making it more widely accessible.

Implementing mechanisms for coordinating international efforts to address AI safety challenges is also crucial for sustaining and enhancing the significance of this international cooperation. These can include international committees, non-profits, and educational institutions that outline the latest guidelines and best practices for everyone to follow. Parallel to that, we can have more formal frameworks, such as international regulations to keep monopolies in check, and other initiatives to foster more collaboration in the corresponding companies regarding AI safety matters.

7.7 Key takeaways

- To address AI safety challenges, we need to develop strategies to detect and mitigate unintended consequences by compiling lists of short-term, medium-term, and long-term effects; establish procedures for reporting and addressing potential safety issues through prioritization, analytics, and proactive problem-solving; and implement mechanisms for tracking and analyzing AI system performance metrics that consider alignment with human values, user feedback, and stakeholder input.

- To mitigate adversarial attacks on AI systems, particularly LLMs, three strategies are necessary: developing techniques for generating intentionally misleading or manipulative input data (adversarial examples), implementing mechanisms for detecting and responding to malicious inputs, and establishing procedures for updating and refining AI system defenses, with a focus on finding a balance between usability and security.

- To improve transparency and explainability in AI systems, three strategies are proposed: developing techniques for generating interpretable models or decision-making processes, implementing mechanisms for providing clear explanations of AI system decisions and outcomes, and establishing procedures for verifying AI system performance and accuracy; these efforts can lead to more robust predictions and decisions, reduced biases and errors, and a better understanding of how AI systems operate.

- We can tackle the issue of fairness and discrimination in AI by developing strategies for ensuring AI safety by detecting and mitigating bias in decision-making processes, implementing mechanisms for fairness and non-discrimination in outcomes, and establishing procedures for reporting and addressing potential safety issues related to fairness and discrimination, all while adapting to changing societal norms and values.

- Developing an ethical framework for AI development and deployment involves defining principles for responsible AI development, establishing procedures for integrating ethical considerations into system design and implementation, and implementing mechanisms for tracking and analyzing performance metrics against ethical standards; this requires a multidisciplinary approach, constant values alignment, and ongoing monitoring to ensure that ethical considerations are integrated into all stages of the AI development process.

- Fostering international cooperation on AI safety requires developing international frameworks for governance and regulation, establishing procedures for sharing knowledge and best practices across borders, and implementing mechanisms for coordinating international efforts to address challenges. This can be achieved through initiatives such as educational programs, conferences, seminars, workshops, competitions, and formal frameworks, including regulations.

CHAPTER 8

The Human and Societal Aspects of AI Safety

8.0 Introduction

While previous chapters have explored the technical foundations of AI safety, we must now focus on the most crucial dimension: the human element. AI systems do not exist in isolation; they are deeply embedded in our social fabric, affecting how we work, interact, and make decisions. This integration presents unprecedented opportunities and complex challenges that extend far beyond technical specifications. From workflow displacement and changes in human behavior to the profound questions of value alignment, the social aspects of AI safety demand our careful attention. In this chapter, we'll explore how organizations and society can proactively address these challenges, ensuring that AI development enhances rather than diminishes human agency and well-being.

8.1 Workforce displacement and job redefinition

While AI promises enhanced productivity and innovation, it also raises important questions about job security, skill requirements, and economic fairness. This section examines practical approaches for managing workforce transitions, promoting human-AI collaboration, and developing inclusive frameworks that support workers during this technological transformation. Our focus is on turning potential displacement into opportunities for growth while maintaining social cohesion and economic stability.

8.1.1 Understanding AI's impact on employment

The relationship between AI and employment is more nuanced than the simple replacement of human workers. We're witnessing a fundamental reshaping of work itself, where AI acts as both a disruptive and creative force in the job market. Traditional roles aren't just disappearing—they're evolving, splitting, or merging into new positions that often require a blend of technical and human skills.

Consider the case of legal professionals. While AI can now review documents and flag potential issues, it hasn't replaced lawyers. Instead, it has created a need for legal experts who understand both law and AI capabilities. These professionals allocate less time to routine document review and more time to complex analysis, client interaction, and strategic decision-making. This pattern repeats across industries: accountants become financial strategists, customer service representatives become complex problem solvers, and manufacturers become robotics operators.

Research suggests that jobs involving repetitive and predictable tasks are at the highest risk of automation. However, this doesn't mean wholesale elimination of positions. In healthcare, for example, AI assists with diagnostic imaging; however, medical professionals remain essential for interpreting results, developing treatment plans, and providing patient care. The technology augments human capabilities rather than replacing them entirely.

The geographic and demographic impact of AI-driven changes varies significantly. Urban areas with high concentrations of technology companies often experience job growth in AI-related fields. In contrast, regions heavily reliant on traditional manufacturing or routine service jobs may face greater challenges. This uneven distribution of opportunities and impacts requires targeted intervention strategies.

New job categories are emerging at a faster rate than ever before. Roles like AI ethics officers, human-AI interaction designers, and automation management specialists didn't exist a decade ago. These positions often combine technical knowledge with traditionally human skills, such as ethical judgment, creativity, and complex problem-solving. Understanding this dynamic helps us better prepare for workforce transitions.

Data from various industries reveal an important pattern: organizations that approach AI adoption as an opportunity for workforce enhancement rather than solely as a cost reduction tend to see better outcomes. These companies typically retain more employees by investing in retraining programs and creating new roles that leverage both human expertise and AI capabilities.

8.1.2 Strategic workforce adaptation and upskilling

Studies show that organizations implementing comprehensive upskilling programs well before AI deployment experience smoother transitions and higher employee retention rates. This forward-looking approach helps build both technical competency and employee confidence. And it's not just a good idea. It's the law. In the EU, every organization is required to provide adequate AI literacy training to its workforce.

Effective upskilling strategies typically operate on three levels: technical literacy, AI interaction skills, and adaptive capabilities. Technical literacy ensures workers understand basic AI concepts and can work with AI-powered tools. Interaction skills enable employees to effectively collaborate with AI systems, knowing both their capabilities and limitations. Adaptive capabilities help workers continuously learn and evolve as technology advances.

Consider the transformation of the banking sector: traditional tellers have evolved into financial advisors who utilize AI-powered tools to deliver personalized customer service. The successful transition required training on new digital platforms, enhanced customer relationship skills, and a deeper understanding of financial products. Banks that invested in comprehensive training programs retained more employees and reported higher customer satisfaction rates.

The development of personalized learning pathways proves more effective than one-size-fits-all approaches. By assessing individual employee skills and career goals, organizations can create targeted training programs that address specific skill gaps while building on existing strengths. This might include a mix of online courses, hands-on workshops, mentoring programs, and real-world project experience.

Critical to success is the timing and pacing of upskilling initiatives. Rolling out training programs too quickly can overwhelm employees, while moving too slowly risks falling behind technological advancements. Organizations that find success typically implement modular training programs, allowing employees to learn incrementally while maintaining their current responsibilities.

The financial investment in upskilling often raises concerns, but data increasingly shows its cost-effectiveness compared to the expenses of hiring and onboarding new employees. Companies that allocate 5-10% of their AI implementation budgets to training programs report smoother transitions and higher returns on investment. These programs often pay for themselves through improved productivity and reduced turnover.

Cross-skilling has emerged as a particularly effective strategy. Instead of focusing solely on technical skills, successful programs help employees develop complementary capabilities. For example, data analysts learn project management skills, while project managers gain data literacy. This creates more versatile employees who can adapt to changing role requirements and take on new responsibilities as they emerge.

Building internal training capacity ensures sustainable skill development. Organizations that establish internal AI expertise centers or partner with educational institutions create ongoing learning opportunities that evolve in response to technological advancements. These centers become hubs for continuous learning and innovation, helping maintain workforce adaptability over time.

8.1.3 Human-AI collaboration models

The future of work isn't about humans competing with AI, but rather about developing effective collaboration models that leverage the strengths of both. We're discovering that the most successful implementations of AI technology create synergistic relationships where human intuition, creativity, emotional intelligence, and complex decision-making complement AI's speed, consistency, and data processing capabilities.

The "AI as tool" model represents the most common form of collaboration currently in practice. Under this framework, AI serves as an advanced instrument that enhances human capabilities rather than replacing them. For example, radiologists utilize AI to flag potential abnormalities in medical images while maintaining control over diagnosis and treatment decisions. This model emphasizes human agency while benefiting from AI's pattern recognition capabilities.

More sophisticated is the "augmented intelligence" approach, where AI systems work alongside humans as intelligent partners. In financial trading, for instance, AI algorithms analyze market trends and suggest trading strategies. At the same time, human traders apply their understanding of broader economic contexts and client relationships to make final decisions. This model creates a dynamic partnership that combines machine efficiency with human judgment.

Organizations are also experimenting with "hybrid teams" where AI systems and human workers have clearly defined, complementary roles. In customer service, AI handles routine inquiries and data collection, allowing human agents to focus on complex problem-solving and emotional support. The key to success lies in clearly defining the boundaries and handoff points between AI and human responsibilities.

The concept of "AI supervision" has emerged as another important model, where humans oversee and guide AI systems while the systems handle routine tasks. This approach is particularly effective in quality control and compliance monitoring, where AI can process vast amounts of data while humans focus on handling exceptions and making strategic decisions. The model emphasizes human accountability while maximizing operational efficiency.

Emerging evidence suggests that successful human-AI collaboration requires careful attention to interface design and workflow integration. Systems that provide clear explanations for their recommendations and maintain transparent decision-making processes tend to foster better cooperation with human workers. This transparency fosters trust and enables workers to make informed decisions about when to rely on AI assistance and when to apply their own judgment.

Training programs for human-AI collaboration need to focus on both technical skills and collaborative competencies. Workers must understand not only how to operate AI tools but also how to partner with them effectively. This includes developing skills in AI oversight, result interpretation, and knowing when to trust or question AI outputs.

8.1.4 Policy frameworks for just transition

A just transition to an AI-augmented workforce necessitates carefully designed policy frameworks that strike a balance between innovation and social responsibility. We're seeing successful approaches emerge that combine regulatory guidelines, economic incentives, and social protection measures to ensure that technological advancements benefit society as a whole.

Corporate responsibility policies are evolving to include specific requirements for AI transition. Organizations above a certain size or in critical sectors are increasingly expected to develop comprehensive transition plans that include worker retraining programs, clear communication strategies, and impact assessments. These policies often mandate minimum investment levels in worker development and establish timelines for the gradual implementation of technology.

Public-private partnerships play a crucial role in creating effective support systems. Government agencies collaborate with businesses and educational institutions to develop regional skill development programs, provide job placement services, and offer transition assistance. For example, some regions have established "Future of Work" centers that combine unemployment support with AI literacy training and job matching services.

Economic safety net provisions need to be updated to address AI-driven changes in employment patterns. Traditional unemployment insurance and worker protection programs are being redesigned to account for partial automation, hybrid roles, and transitional employment periods. This includes developing new categories of benefits for workers in retraining programs and those transitioning between traditional and AI-augmented roles.

Educational system alignment has become a critical policy focus. Updating curriculum standards at all levels to include AI literacy and adaptive skills helps prepare the future workforce while providing retraining opportunities for current workers. Some jurisdictions now require educational institutions to regularly update their programs based on AI impact assessments and projected skill needs.

Small business support frameworks deserve special attention in policy design. While larger organizations can often manage transition costs internally, smaller businesses need structured support to adapt to AI technologies without compromising their workforce. Tax incentives, technical assistance programs, and subsidized training initiatives help level the playing field.

Regional development policies increasingly incorporate AI transition planning. Areas identified as high-risk for AI-driven displacement receive targeted support through infrastructure investment, business development incentives, and workforce programs. These policies aim to prevent regional economic decline by proactively building new economic opportunities as traditional jobs evolve.

Stakeholder participation mechanisms ensure policies reflect diverse needs and perspectives. Successful frameworks include regular consultation with workers, employers, educators, and community representatives. This collaborative approach helps identify potential problems early and ensures that support measures address real needs rather than assumed ones.

8.2 AI-driven changes in human behavior

As artificial intelligence becomes increasingly woven into the fabric of daily life, we're observing profound shifts in human behavior, cognition, and social interaction patterns. These changes extend far beyond simple tool usage—they represent fundamental shifts in how we think, make decisions, and interact with both technology and one another. Understanding and responsibly managing these behavioral impacts has emerged as a critical challenge for organizations implementing AI systems, particularly under frameworks like the EU AI Act, which explicitly recognizes the need to protect human agency and psychological well-being.

8.2.1 Cognitive and decision-making patterns

Integrating AI systems into decision-making processes fundamentally alters how humans process information and arrive at conclusions. While AI tools can enhance our cognitive capabilities, they also risk creating problematic dependencies or distorting our natural decision-making processes (also see chapter 3.9 on human-computer interaction. Under the EU AI Act, organizations must actively monitor and mitigate these cognitive impacts, particularly in high-risk domains where impaired human judgment could have serious consequences.

Consider how AI-powered recommendation systems have transformed professional decision-making. A financial advisor utilizing AI-driven market analysis tools may process significantly more data than previously possible. Still, this capability raises important questions: How does constant exposure to AI-generated recommendations affect human intuition and expertise? When does enhanced information processing cross the line into cognitive overdependence?

Research reveals several key patterns in AI-influenced decision-making:

- **Anchoring Effects**: When AI systems provide initial recommendations, human decision-makers often display a strong anchoring bias toward these suggestions, even when they have the authority and expertise to disagree. In medical diagnosis, for instance, physicians may hesitate to deviate from AI recommendations even when their clinical experience suggests a different approach.
- **Automation Complacency**: Regular interaction with highly reliable AI systems can lead to a reduction in vigilance and critical thinking. This effect becomes particularly concerning in safety-critical environments, such as air traffic control or industrial operations, where maintaining human oversight is crucial.

These cognitive shifts demand proactive management strategies. Organizations implementing AI decision support systems should consider this framework for preserving healthy human judgment:

- Implement mandatory cooling-off periods for critical decisions
- Rotate between AI-assisted and traditional decision-making approaches
- Design interfaces that actively prompt critical evaluation
- Structure workflows to require explicit reasoning before accepting AI recommendations
- Have AI systems output counterfactuals—what would be needed to change the decision, rather than what substantiated it?

Legal frameworks, particularly the EU AI Act, require organizations to maintain meaningful human oversight in AI-supported decisions. This translates into practical requirements for system design and operational procedures, such as ensuring a clear presentation of confidence levels and uncertainty ranges, explicitly flagging assumptions and limitations, and allowing for independent human assessment. A particularly effective strategy is to request a human assessment before displaying the AI output. This activates human judgment.

Training programs must evolve to develop "AI-aware cognition"—the ability to effectively leverage AI insights while maintaining independent judgment. This includes teaching professionals to recognize their own cognitive biases in AI interaction, maintain domain expertise independent of AI tools and document decision rationales, especially when deviating from AI suggestions.

High-stakes decisions require particularly robust approaches to maintaining cognitive independence when working with AI systems. Validation processes that help decision-makers maintain their autonomy while benefiting from AI insights typically begin with an independent human assessment before any AI consultation, ensuring that AI suggestions don't initially anchor professional judgment. Next, decision-makers can engage with AI recommendations and supporting data. This staged approach helps prevent the common pitfall of cognitive anchoring, where early exposure to AI suggestions might unduly influence human judgment. The key is creating space for genuine critical analysis, where professionals can systematically compare their independent conclusions with those generated by AI.

Documentation plays a crucial role in this process, particularly under the EU AI Act's requirements for transparency and accountability. Decision-makers must clearly articulate their reasoning, especially in cases where they deviate from AI recommendations. This documentation serves multiple purposes: it creates an audit trail for compliance, provides data for system improvement, and helps professionals maintain awareness of their own decision-making patterns.

Organizations find that maintaining systematic feedback loops significantly enhances the quality of human-AI decision-making over time. Regular reviews of decision outcomes help refine both the AI systems and the validation processes themselves. These reviews often reveal patterns that may not be apparent in individual cases—for instance, identifying situations where human oversight is particularly crucial or where AI support could be more effectively integrated into the decision-making process.

The transition toward AI-augmented cognition requires careful attention to professional development and skill maintenance. Organizations must ensure that reliance on AI tools doesn't erode core competencies. This might involve regular "AI-free" exercises where professionals practice traditional decision-making methods to maintain fundamental skills.

8.2.2 Social interaction and communication changes

Digital communication environments increasingly feature AI-powered elements that subtly shape human interaction patterns. From automated content suggestions to sentiment analysis tools, these systems don't merely facilitate communication—they actively influence its nature and direction. Consider how AI-powered email systems now suggest responses, timing, and tone adjustments. While these features can enhance efficiency, they also raise crucial questions about authenticity and agency in professional communication.

Research into AI-mediated social interactions reveals emerging patterns that demand careful consideration. Professional environments that utilize AI communication tools report increased efficiency, but also note subtle shifts in relationship dynamics. For instance, when AI systems flag potential conflicts in written communication, they can prevent misunderstandings but may also create overly cautious communication patterns that diminish authentic human connection.

AI systems are also influencing the temporal patterns of human interaction. Real-time sentiment analysis and automated scheduling tools create new expectations for response speed and availability. While these tools can enhance coordination, organizations report that they may also contribute to communication pressure and reduced reflection time. This presents a direct challenge to workplace well-being provisions under various regulatory frameworks.

To address these challenges, organizations are developing integrated approaches to managing AI-mediated communication:

- Professional interaction guidelines now explicitly address the role of AI tools in workplace communication. These frameworks emphasize maintaining authentic human connections while leveraging AI capabilities appropriately. For instance, customer service teams may use AI to enhance response efficiency while preserving human judgment in emotionally charged or complex situations.
- The preservation of genuine human connection requires careful attention to communication channel design. Organizations find success by creating clear boundaries between AI-augmented and direct human communication. This might involve designating specific contexts where AI assistance is appropriate while preserving spaces for unmediated human interaction.

- Training programs increasingly focus on developing "AI-aware communication skills." These programs help professionals understand when and how to leverage AI communication tools while maintaining their authentic voice. This includes teaching awareness of AI-induced communication biases and strategies for maintaining genuine human connections in digitally mediated environments.

Cultural adaptation to AI-mediated communication requires ongoing assessment and adjustment. Organizations must regularly evaluate how communication patterns evolve and ensure that efficiency gains don't come at the cost of meaningful human interaction. This involves monitoring both quantitative metrics, such as response times, and qualitative factors, including relationship quality and team cohesion.

8.2.3 Attention and information processing

Research reveals emerging patterns in attention dynamics influenced by AI. Professional environments using AI-powered information systems undergo significant changes in how workers engage with complex information. For instance, financial analysts using AI-driven market intelligence platforms process larger volumes of data, but show measurable changes in the depth of their analysis and retention patterns. These shifts carry important implications for both operational effectiveness and regulatory compliance.

The legal framework surrounding attention protection creates specific obligations for organizations deploying AI systems. Under current regulations, organizations must:

- Monitor and mitigate attention fragmentation risks
- Ensure transparency in AI-driven information prioritization
- Protect user agency in information consumption patterns
- Maintain clear documentation of attention impact assessments.

Organizations implementing AI information systems find that attention management requires a multi-layered approach. Professional environments must strike a balance between the benefits of enhanced information processing and the preservation of sustained attention capabilities. This involves designing workflows that respect cognitive limitations while leveraging AI capabilities to reduce information overload.

The impact on long-term cognitive development presents particular challenges for organizational policy. Extended exposure to AI-mediated information environments may fundamentally alter how professionals develop and maintain expertise. While AI tools can accelerate initial learning, organizations report that they may also affect the development of deep analytical skills that traditionally emerge through sustained engagement with complex information.

To address these challenges, organizations are developing integrated frameworks for attention management. These approaches typically combine technological design, policy implementation, and ongoing monitoring:

- Information environment design now explicitly considers cognitive load and attention dynamics. Organizations implement features like mandatory reflection periods, structured information hierarchies, and clear context switches to protect cognitive resources. These design elements help maintain compliance with regulatory requirements while supporting effective information processing.
- Training programs increasingly emphasize "attention literacy" as a core professional competency. These initiatives help workers understand their own attention patterns and develop strategies for maintaining cognitive effectiveness in AI-augmented environments. This includes techniques for managing information flow, recognizing attention fatigue, and maintaining critical thinking capabilities.
- Monitoring systems track both immediate and long-term impacts on attention patterns. Organizations utilize sophisticated analytics to detect potentially harmful changes in information processing behaviors while ensuring compliance with relevant privacy regulations. This data helps refine system design and inform policy adjustments while maintaining transparency about AI's role in information flow.

Organizations must prepare for increasingly sophisticated AI information processing capabilities while ensuring robust protection of human cognitive capacities. This includes developing clear policies for the use of AI in information curation, establishing boundaries for automated processing, and maintaining transparency regarding AI involvement in information flows.

Of particular interest is the rising phenomenon of the "AI-free periods"—designated timeframes where teams operate without AI assistance to maintain independent cognitive skills and prevent overdependence. These might take the form of "AI-free Fridays" (biweekly), dedicated deep work sessions, or regular "analog sprints" for specific projects. Organizations implementing these practices report multiple benefits: preserved independent thinking capabilities, enhanced team creativity when facing novel challenges, and stronger critical assessment skills when AI systems are reintroduced.

8.2.4 Behavioral dependencies and digital habits

When professionals rely on AI systems for routine tasks, gradual shifts in decision-making autonomy emerge. Consider how AI-powered productivity tools, while enhancing efficiency, can create persistent dependencies that may compromise professional judgment over time. Organizations report increasing instances of "AI consultation reflex"—where professionals automatically defer to AI systems even in situations where human judgment should prevail. This phenomenon carries particular significance in regulated industries where maintaining meaningful human oversight isn't merely good practice but a legal requirement.

To address these challenges, organizations must implement comprehensive frameworks for dependency prevention that align with both their technological capabilities and legal obligations. This requires careful attention to several key domains:

- System design plays a crucial role in preventing harmful dependencies. Organizations find success by implementing features that actively promote user agency and conscious engagement. This includes mandatory reflection periods before critical decisions, clear indicators of AI system limitations, and structured opportunities for independent human judgment. These design elements help maintain compliance with regulatory requirements while fostering healthy human-AI interaction patterns.

- Professional development and AI literacy programs increasingly emphasize "digital resilience" as a core competency. These initiatives help workers develop robust strategies for maintaining autonomy while effectively leveraging AI capabilities. Training focuses on recognizing signs of over-consideration of AI systems, developing confident, independent judgment, and maintaining professional skills that complement rather than defer to AI capabilities.

The legal framework surrounding behavioral dependencies imposes specific obligations on organizations that deploy AI systems. The EU AI Act refers to this as the "AI literacy obligation." The aim is to ensure that users have an appropriate level of understanding and competency. This translates into specific organizational requirements:

- Technical Literacy
  - Documented training programs explaining AI system capabilities and limitations
  - Regular assessments of user understanding of AI system functionality
  - Clear protocols for identifying and addressing knowledge gaps
  - Maintained records of AI literacy assessments and interventions.

- Behavioral Competency
  - Structured monitoring of interaction patterns with AI systems
  - Regular evaluation of decision-making independence
  - Documentation of dependency risk assessments
  - Implementation of early warning systems for problematic usage patterns.

- Professional Development
  - Integration of AI literacy into broader professional qualification frameworks
  - Regular skill maintenance programs emphasizing human expertise
  - Clear pathways for developing complementary capabilities
  - Documented strategies for maintaining professional judgment.

Monitoring systems must evolve beyond simple usage metrics to track subtle indicators of behavioral dependency. Organizations are implementing sophisticated analytics that examine patterns of AI system interaction, decision-making processes, and professional skill maintenance. This data helps identify potential dependencies before they become problematic while ensuring compliance with privacy regulations and worker protection frameworks. This involves careful attention to system design, ongoing monitoring, and regular assessment of interaction patterns to ensure alignment with both regulatory requirements and professional development goals.

8.3 Trust and transparency

Building justified trust through meaningful transparency has emerged as both a legal imperative and operational necessity. This is, in fact, one of the cornerstones of the EU's AI strategy, referring to "trustworthy AI" as the baseline for regulating artificial intelligence. AI systems are considered trustworthy if they can demonstrate that they can be trusted. Transparency on their inner workings, the quality of their data, and the explanations of their output are three key aspects.

8.3.1 Building foundations for AI system verification

The foundation of trust in AI systems rests on our ability to verify their performance against clear, measurable standards. Under the EU AI Act, organizations must implement systematic verification processes that demonstrate both technical reliability and legal compliance. This verification framework extends beyond simple accuracy metrics to encompass fairness, consistency, and alignment with fundamental rights.

Consider an AI system used in loan approval decisions. Traditional verification might focus solely on prediction accuracy, but comprehensive verification must go beyond that. Trust also requires a level of robustness against data variations and edge cases, and the ability to rely on system stability across different operational conditions. The manner and level of human oversight add a further level of trustworthiness.

Organizations implementing these verification frameworks typically begin with a baseline assessment that maps system capabilities against relevant legal requirements. A practical approach involves creating verification matrices that connect technical metrics directly to legal obligations. For example:

Technical Metric	EU AI Act Requirement	Verification Method
Decision consistency	Art. 15 reliability	Controlled A/B testing
Protected group fairness	Art. 10.2 bias prevention	Demographics analysis
Error rate distribution	Art. 15 accuracy	Continuous monitoring
Oversight effectiveness	Art. 13 transparency	Human feedback loops

Real-world implementation requires careful attention to both procedural and substantive verification. While procedural verification ensures proper documentation and process adherence, substantive verification examines actual system behavior and outcomes. Organizations successful in building trusted AI systems typically implement a three-phase verification approach:

- Pre-deployment Verification
    - Comprehensive testing against predefined benchmarks
    - Adversarial testing to identify potential failure modes
    - Stakeholder consultation and impact assessment
    - Documentation of baseline performance metrics.

- Operational Verification
    - Real-time monitoring of key performance indicators
    - Regular audits of decision patterns and outcomes
    - Continuous feedback collection from human operators
    - Systematic error analysis and classification.

- Periodic Deep Verification
    - Comprehensive system behavior analysis
    - Update impact assessments
    - Regulatory compliance reviews
    - Stakeholder experience evaluation.

The verification process must adapt to the system's risk level and application context. High-risk applications, as defined under the EU AI Act, require more rigorous verification protocols. For instance, AI systems in healthcare diagnostics need verification processes that examine not just technical accuracy but also clinical relevance, diagnostic consistency, and integration with existing medical protocols.

Emerging best practices suggest that effective verification systems incorporate feedback loops that connect technical metrics with real-world outcomes. This might involve tracking not just system performance but also user trust levels, operational efficiency, and unintended consequences. Organizations find that this holistic approach to verification helps identify potential issues before they become significant problems while building justified trust among stakeholders.

8.3.2 Transparency in AI decision processes

A challenge for many organizations is making complex decision processes transparent without overwhelming users or compromising system efficiency. What is "sufficiently transparent"? The EU AI Act has this as a legal requirement, yet does not elaborate on how to establish the required level. Let's examine how this legal requirement translates into practical implementation through a layered transparency framework.

First, organizations must document and communicate how AI systems move from input to output. Consider a recruitment AI system—rather than presenting decisions as final verdicts, the system should reveal its evaluation pathway:

Traditional Approach	Transparent Approach
"Candidate match: 85%"	"Skills alignment (40%), Experience fit (30%), Education match (15%)"
"Application rejected"	"Areas for consideration: Project experience below threshold, Technical certifications pending"

Having established this baseline level of transparency, the next level is to add clarity about what data influences decisions. Organizations implement this through:

- Clear data lineage documentation
- Explicit identification of data sources
- Regular data quality assessments
- Accessible data retention policies.

Going one step further, organizations must provide meaningful insights into system capabilities and limitations. This typically involves:

- Documented model cards describing key characteristics
- Performance boundaries and confidence levels
- Known limitations and edge cases
- Regular capability assessments.

Real-world implementation requires balancing competing interests. Consider how different stakeholders interact with AI transparency:

Stakeholder	Transparency Need	Implementation Strategy
End Users	Understanding decisions	Layered explanations with progressive detail
Operators	System oversight capability	Technical dashboards with real-time monitoring
Auditors	Compliance verification	Comprehensive documentation and audit trails
Regulators	Legal compliance evidence	Structured reporting aligned with requirements

Organizations successful in implementing transparency frameworks typically follow a staged approach:

Stage 1: Foundation Building
- Establish baseline transparency requirements
- Map legal obligations to system capabilities
- Create initial documentation framework
- Develop stakeholder communication plans.

Stage 2: Implementation
- Deploy transparency mechanisms
- Train staff on transparency tools
- Establish monitoring protocols
- Begin collecting user feedback.

Stage 3: Refinement
- Analyze transparency effectiveness
- Adjust based on stakeholder feedback
- Enhance documentation quality
- Optimize communication methods.

The key to effective transparency lies in making complex processes understandable without oversimplification. For instance, rather than merely stating, "Diagnosis suggested based on AI analysis," a provider may point to the fact that 1,500+ similar cases were analyzed, comparisons with current clinical guidelines gave good results, and consideration of patient history gave a confidence level of 85%. This approach satisfies legal requirements while providing practical utility for healthcare professionals. Organizations must remember that transparency isn't just about disclosure—it's about enabling informed decision-making and meaningful oversight. Section 4.3 provides more information.

8.3.3 Creating meaningful explanations

Opening up the "black box" that most AI represents has been a challenge for many deployers of AI systems in the past years. With the EU AI Act in particular this has become a legal requirement, with other jurisdictions—Brazil, South Africa, South Korea—following in its footsteps. Data protection legislation also often contains provisions requiring algorithmic decision-making to be accompanied by a motivation or explanation. More generally, most countries' laws provide that decisions by government agencies are sufficiently substantiated. And of course "the AI has rejected your welfare application" is not a substantiation. So how to arrive at meaningful explanations?

A structured approach to meaningful explanations typically encompasses three key dimensions: contextual relevance, accessibility and actionable intelligence. On relevance, explanations must adapt to both user role and decision context:

Decision Type	Explanation Focus	Implementation Example
Time-Critical	Key factors and confidence level	Emergency response triage: "High risk assessment (92% confidence) based on vital signs and response time"
Strategic	Comprehensive analysis with alternatives	Investment recommendation: "Market volatility analysis suggests defensive position, supported by three key economic indicators..."
Routine	Streamlined explanation with escalation path	Document classification: "Flagged as sensitive due to personal data content, requiring supervisor review"

Keeping accessibility and inclusivity in mind, organizations should implement tiered explanation systems that satisfy different stakeholder needs:

Layer	Purpose	Content Type
Overview	Quick understanding	Visual indicators, summary statements
Standard	Operational use	Key factors, confidence levels, main alternatives
Detailed	Technical/legal review	Complete decision path, data lineage, model parameters

Lastly, explanations must enable informed decision-making. This requires providing actionable information, often including recommended next steps or pointing at the likely origin of problematic issues. In the context of legal decisions, such as when rejecting job applicants or evaluating public assistance applications, this translates to a requirement to identify those issues most influential on the outcome.

Traditional Approach	Enhanced Approach
"Risk score: 7.5/10"	"Risk factors: Supply chain disruption (40%), Market volatility (35%), Regulatory changes (25%)—Recommended actions provided"
"Anomaly detected"	"Unusual pattern in financial transactions—Compare with baseline metrics and regulatory thresholds"
"Application status: Not selected for position."	"Application Review Results: Key Qualification Gaps: • Required technical certification missing (Impact: 40%) • Project management experience below threshold (Impact: 35%) • Language proficiency requirements not met (Impact: 25%)"

The effectiveness of explanations often hinges on finding the right balance between completeness and clarity. Consider this evolution in explanation design:

Version 1 (Too Technical): " Model output indicates 73% probability based on deep neural network analysis with attention mechanisms across 15 input variables processed through three hidden layers..."

Version 2 (Too Vague): "System suggests approval based on overall assessment..."

Version 3 (Balanced): "Recommendation: Approve Key Factors:

- Payment history (consistent over 24 months)
- Income verification (exceeds threshold by 40%)
- Risk assessment (low, based on industry standards) Action Options: Approve as recommended, Request additional verification, or Escalate for review."

8.3.4 Trust through continuous monitoring

Trust in AI systems emerges from consistently demonstrating reliable, fair, and transparent operation over time—much like trust in human institutions develops through sustained accountability and proven performance, as with financial auditors that oversee corporate operations. This approach reflects a deeper understanding that trust, once earned, must be actively maintained through systematic oversight and transparent accountability.

The operational dimension demands particular attention, as it bridges technical performance with real-world impact. Organizations must assess how effectively AI systems integrate with business processes, how successfully human oversight mechanisms function, and how readily exceptions are handled. This holistic view enables early detection of potential issues before they manifest as compliance violations or operational disruptions. Consider how this framework applies to a financial services AI system:

Monitoring Dimension	Traditional Approach	Enhanced Approach (EU AI Act Compliant)
Performance Tracking	Monthly accuracy reports	Real-time monitoring with automated alerts for drift detection
Compliance Verification	Annual audits	Continuous compliance scanning with daily validation checks
Impact Assessment	Quarterly reviews	Dynamic impact tracking with stakeholder feedback integration

Successful implementation requires both proactive and reactive capabilities. Proactive monitoring employs drift detection algorithms, automated fairness checks, and regular validation testing to identify potential issues before they impact operations. Reactive monitoring provides structured incident response protocols and investigation workflows to address issues that may arise. This dual approach ensures organizations can both prevent problems and respond effectively when necessary.

Organizations must establish clear governance structures and response protocols to address potential issues identified through monitoring. The most effective approaches implement tiered alert levels with corresponding response requirements:

Alert Level	Response Protocol	Documentation Requirements
Advisory	System review within 24 hours	Internal incident report
Warning	Immediate human oversight activation	Detailed investigation log
Critical	System pause and stakeholder notification	Comprehensive compliance review

Maintaining effective monitoring systems requires robust communication channels between technical, legal, and operational stakeholders. Clear protocols must govern alert notifications, stakeholder updates, and escalation pathways. Documentation plays a crucial role, with comprehensive logs maintaining records of monitoring activities, investigations, and resolution actions. This documentation serves both operational needs and compliance requirements, providing evidence of ongoing oversight and system governance.

8.4 Value alignment

Value alignment represents the most fundamental challenge in AI safety—ensuring that artificial intelligence systems not only function effectively but also operate in harmony with human values, ethical principles, and societal norms. The EU AI Act was built on value alignment, identifying seven core values that reflect the region's fundamental rights. In this section, we explore practical frameworks for identifying value conflicts, establishing verification procedures, and implementing mechanisms that ensure AI development remains anchored to human well-being and dignity.

8.4.1 Identifying and managing value conflicts

Value conflicts between AI systems and human priorities (see section 3.1) emerge in subtle yet significant ways that can profoundly impact organizational operations and societal trust. Consider an AI system deployed in healthcare resource allocation. While the system may optimize for quantifiable metrics such as bed utilization and treatment costs, it may inadvertently conflict with human values regarding equitable access and individualized care. For instance, a purely efficiency-driven algorithm might consistently disadvantage patients with complex conditions requiring longer recovery times, creating tension between operational efficiency and healthcare equity. These conflicts often manifest across three primary dimensions: procedural values (how decisions should be made), substantive values (what outcomes matter), and instrumental values (which methods are acceptable). An AI recruitment system may excel at identifying candidates based on past performance metrics but struggle with evaluating human values such as potential, personal growth, and workplace diversity. The EU AI Act specifically addresses this through requirements for human oversight and the protection of fundamental rights, mandating that organizations implement mechanisms to detect and resolve such conflicts.

Real-world implementation necessitates that organizations develop structured frameworks for assessing value conflicts. This process begins with systematic value mapping, which involves documenting both explicit organizational values and the implicit assumptions embedded in AI systems. When a major financial institution implemented an AI-driven customer service system, it first created a comprehensive value matrix comparing its stated commitment to personalized customer relationships against the automated efficiency gains promised by the AI system. This proactive approach helped identify potential conflicts before deployment, allowing for system adjustments that preserved both efficiency and relationship quality.

Organizations must also consider temporal aspects of value alignment. Values and priorities can shift over time, necessitating that AI systems adapt accordingly. The EU AI Act's requirement for regular system assessments reflects this reality, pushing organizations to implement dynamic monitoring systems that track value alignment as an ongoing process rather than a one-time certification. For instance, a smart city traffic management system might need to evolve from purely efficiency-based routing to incorporate emerging community values around environmental impact and neighborhood preservation.

Effective conflict management requires clear escalation pathways and resolution frameworks. When value conflicts arise, organizations need established protocols for assessment and intervention. Consider this progressive approach implemented by a large insurance provider:

Value Conflict Level	Response Protocol	Documentation Requirements
Minor Misalignment	System adjustment within operational parameters	Internal review report
Significant Tension	Human oversight activation and system constraints	Detailed impact assessment
Critical Conflict	System pause and stakeholder consultation	Comprehensive alignment review

The resolution of value conflicts often requires careful balancing of competing interests. Organizations successful in managing these challenges typically employ structured dialogue processes that bring together technical teams, ethics specialists, and stakeholders affected by AI decisions. This collaborative approach helps ensure that technical solutions align with human values while maintaining system effectiveness.

Professional development plays a crucial role in building an organization's capacity for managing value conflicts. Technical teams require training to identify potential value misalignments in system design and operation, while management needs tools to evaluate and address these conflicts from both technical and ethical perspectives. This dual capability enables organizations to maintain compliance with regulatory requirements while fostering trust among stakeholders. Moreover, successful value alignment requires transparency about how conflicts are identified and resolved. Organizations must document not just the technical aspects of conflict resolution but also the reasoning behind their approaches. This documentation serves multiple purposes: demonstrating regulatory compliance, building stakeholder trust, and creating institutional knowledge for future system development.

Emerging practice suggests that forward-looking organizations are moving beyond reactive monitoring toward predictive approaches to value alignment. These organizations can anticipate potential value conflicts before they manifest by applying sophisticated predictive analytics to system behavior, usage patterns, and societal trends. This allows for preemptive adjustments to system parameters, governance frameworks, and stakeholder engagement strategies.

8.4.2 Verification procedures for value alignment

While technical metrics can validate system performance, verifying alignment with human values requires more nuanced approaches that bridge quantitative assessment with qualitative human judgment. The foundation rests on establishing clear assessment criteria that connect abstract values to measurable outcomes. Consider how a financial institution implementing AI-driven loan assessment must verify alignment with both operational efficiency and social responsibility values. Their verification framework might examine not just approval rates and risk metrics, but also patterns of financial inclusion and long-term community impact.

Real-world implementation demands structured verification protocols that can withstand both regulatory scrutiny and stakeholder examination. Organizations successful in this domain typically implement a three-tier verification framework:

Foundational Verification	Operational Verification	Impact Verification
Value principle documentation	Decision pattern analysis	Community impact assessment
Baseline alignment testing	Real-time monitoring systems	Stakeholder feedback integration
Technical constraint validation	Exception handling review	Long-term outcome tracking

The evolution of verification methodologies reflects a growing understanding that value alignment cannot be reduced to simple checklist compliance. Organizations must develop dynamic verification systems that adapt to emerging values and changing societal expectations. A healthcare AI system, for instance, might initially verify alignment through medical outcome metrics but evolve to incorporate broader measures of patient experience and healthcare equity.

Verification procedures must also address the temporal dimension of value alignment. The EU AI Act's requirement for ongoing monitoring recognizes that value alignment is not a static achievement but a continuous process. Organizations implement rolling verification schedules that examine system behavior across different timeframes and contexts. This might involve regular assessment points, triggered reviews based on operational thresholds, and comprehensive periodic audits that examine long-term patterns and outcomes.

Professional capacity for verifying value alignment requires specialized training that combines technical expertise with ethical awareness. Organizations develop verification teams that can navigate both quantitative metrics and qualitative assessments, understanding how technical parameters translate into real-world impact. This dual competency enables more effective verification processes to identify subtle misalignments before they manifest as significant problems.

The integration of stakeholder perspectives into verification procedures has emerged as a crucial element of effective value alignment. Organizations implement structured feedback mechanisms that capture diverse viewpoints on the system's impact and effectiveness of alignment. This might involve regular consultations with affected communities, expert panel reviews, and systematic analysis of user experiences. The insights gained help refine verification criteria, ensuring that alignment assessments reflect the real-world impact.

8.4.3 Implementing human-centric development frameworks

Development frameworks must systematically incorporate human-centric principles while maintaining technical rigor and operational efficiency. Consider how a major healthcare provider implemented AI diagnostic support tools. Rather than focusing solely on medical accuracy, their development framework explicitly incorporated patient autonomy, cultural sensitivity, and metrics related to healthcare equity. A financial services AI system implemented a framework that allows for the evaluation of each development decision against its impact on financial inclusion, customer autonomy, and long-term economic well-being.

Translating human-centric principles into development practices requires careful attention to both process and outcome. Professional development teams thus must cultivate new competencies that bridge technical expertise with human-centric considerations. This involves training in ethical impact assessment, stakeholder engagement, and human rights implications of technical decisions. Organizations find that cross-functional teams incorporating diverse perspectives—technical, ethical, legal, and social—produce more robust human-centric solutions. These teams can better anticipate potential impacts on human dignity and agency while maintaining technical excellence.

Real-world implementation demands practical mechanisms for validating human-centricity throughout the development lifecycle. Consider this evolution in development checkpoints implemented by a major public service organization:

Development Stage	Traditional Approach	Human-Centric Approach
Requirements Gathering	Technical specifications focus	Integration of human impact assessment
Design Phase	Efficiency optimization	Balance of efficiency with human agency
Testing Protocol	Functional validation	Comprehensive human impact validation
Deployment Strategy	Technical rollout plan	Staged deployment with human oversight
Monitoring Framework	Performance metrics	Human-centric impact indicators

The documentation of human-centric development decisions serves both operational and compliance purposes. Organizations must maintain clear records demonstrating how human considerations influence technical choices. This documentation becomes particularly crucial under the EU AI Act's requirements for transparency and accountability, as it provides evidence that human dignity and agency were properly considered throughout the development process.

Stakeholder engagement takes on heightened importance within human-centric frameworks. Organizations must implement structured processes to incorporate diverse perspectives throughout the development process. This might involve regular consultations with affected communities, expert ethics panels, and systematic feedback loops that capture real-world impact on human well-being. These insights refine development approaches, ensuring that solutions truly serve human needs. The evolution of human-centric development frameworks must also address emerging challenges around AI autonomy and decision-making authority. Organizations increasingly implement graduated autonomy protocols that balance AI capabilities with human oversight requirements. This approach helps maintain compliance with regulatory frameworks while ensuring that AI systems enhance, rather than diminish, human agency. By anchoring development in human-centric principles, organizations can create AI systems that not only meet technical specifications but actively contribute to human flourishing. This aligns with both regulatory requirements and emerging societal expectations about responsible AI development, creating a foundation for sustainable technological advancement that respects and enhances human dignity.

8.4.4 Cultural and ethical considerations in value alignment

The intersection of cultural diversity and AI value alignment presents one of the most nuanced challenges in modern technological governance. Organizations must navigate a complex landscape where cultural values and ethical frameworks vary significantly across societies and contexts. This extends beyond simple localization or regional adaptation. Consider how a global healthcare AI system must navigate diverse cultural perspectives on privacy, familial involvement in medical decisions, and end-of-life care. Of particular concern is the fact that many AI systems originate from Western, Educated, Industrialized, Rich, and Democratic or *WEIRD* countries. A term coined by Joseph Henrich indicates that such systems have inherent cultural biases that can profoundly impact their global deployment and effectiveness. For instance, consider how AI systems handling financial risk assessment might embed Western concepts of individual creditworthiness that clash with collective financial responsibility systems common in many non-Western societies. AI systems designed for healthcare decision support often prioritize individual patient autonomy. This characteristically Western approach may conflict with the family-centered medical decision-making that is common in many Asian and African cultures. More generally, many AI systems categorize people or objects into distinct categories and assign properties to account for their behavior, which is a fundamentally WEIRD phenomenon.

Ethical frameworks for AI value alignment must evolve beyond such Western-centric paradigms to incorporate diverse philosophical traditions and moral systems. Organizations successful in this domain implement what we might call "culturally adaptive ethics frameworks"—structured approaches that maintain core ethical principles while accommodating cultural variation in their expression and implementation. For instance, a financial services AI system might maintain consistent standards for fairness and transparency while adapting its communication methods and explanations of decisions to align with local cultural norms and expectations.

The temporal dimension of cultural values adds another layer of complexity to efforts aimed at alignment. Cultural values evolve over time, often at different rates across societies. Organizations must implement monitoring systems capable of detecting shifts in cultural values that may affect the alignment of AI systems. This dynamic approach aligns with the EU AI Act's requirement for continuous assessment and adaptation of high-risk AI systems. Consider how a global technology company implements culturally sensitive value alignment:

Cultural Dimension	Alignment Strategy	Validation Method
Communication Norms	Adaptive explanation frameworks	Cultural context testing
Decision-Making Models	Flexible oversight structures	Local stakeholder validation
Privacy Expectations	Layered protection protocols	Community feedback systems
Ethical Priorities	Context-sensitive frameworks	Cross-cultural impact assessment

The professional development requirements for cultural competency in AI value alignment present unique challenges. Organizations must build teams capable of understanding and navigating diverse cultural contexts while maintaining technical excellence and legal compliance. This often involves creating cross-cultural training programs that combine technical expertise with anthropological insights and ethical awareness. Stakeholder engagement assumes heightened importance when addressing the cultural dimensions of value alignment. Organizations must implement structured processes to incorporate diverse cultural perspectives throughout the system lifecycle. This might involve regular consultations with cultural experts, community leaders, and affected populations across different societies. These insights refine alignment approaches, ensuring AI systems respect and support cultural diversity. Resolving conflicts between different cultural values and legal requirements demands careful attention to both principle and pragmatism. Organizations must develop structured frameworks for identifying and addressing such conflicts while maintaining compliance with applicable regulations. This might involve creating tiered decision-making protocols that delineate between universal principles and culturally adaptive elements.

8.5 How would you ensure ethical AI implementation in recruitment?

TalentMatch Technologies has developed an AI-powered recruitment system that promises to revolutionize the hiring process for its enterprise clients. The system analyzes resumes, cover letters, and video interviews to generate candidate rankings and recommendations. Their marketing emphasizes the system's ability to "eliminate human bias" and "identify top talent with 95%

accuracy." The current implementation processes application materials and generates a comprehensive candidate score based on factors including keyword matching, educational background, previous employers, work history patterns, and communication style during video interviews. A simple dashboard shows hiring managers the candidates ranked from highest to lowest score, along with a brief explanation stating, "This candidate scored 87/100 based on our proprietary algorithm." After six months of deployment at several client companies, TalentMatch has collected feedback that reveals potential issues. Many hiring managers report a complete reliance on the system's rankings, rarely interviewing candidates who fall below a certain threshold. Some clients have noticed that their new hires seem increasingly homogeneous in terms of background and approach. Additionally, rejected candidates frequently request more information about why they weren't selected, but hiring managers struggle to provide meaningful explanations beyond the numerical score. TalentMatch executives are concerned about potential legal and ethical implications. They've recently learned about forthcoming regulations that would require explainability and fairness in automated hiring systems. They want to ensure their product enhances human decision-making while respecting candidate dignity and promoting diversity.

How would you tackle these ethical concerns? For instance, how would you design an explanation mechanism that provides both hiring managers and candidates with meaningful insights without overwhelming them with technical details? Develop a framework for maintaining human oversight and judgment in the recruitment process. How would you structure the human-AI collaboration to leverage both strengths? Create a monitoring plan to help TalentMatch detect potential value conflicts or misalignments between the system's operation and human values, such as fairness, diversity, and respect for individuals. Consider how the system might inadvertently encode Western cultural assumptions about what makes an "ideal candidate." How would you modify the system to accommodate diverse cultural expressions of professional competence and workplace values?

8.6 Key takeaways

- **Intent Verification Creates Operational Safety**: Ensuring mutual understanding between humans and AI systems transcends simple confirmation dialogues to encompass structured mechanisms that verify comprehension on both sides. Organizations must implement verification protocols proportionate to decision stakes—from simple undo functions for low-risk tasks to comprehensive validation procedures for high-consequence applications.

- **Workforce Transformation Demands Strategic Management**: AI's impact on employment isn't a simple replacement narrative but a fundamental reshaping of work itself, creating roles that blend technical and human capabilities. Organizations that implement comprehensive reskilling programs before AI deployment experience higher retention rates and smoother transitions, particularly when developing personalized learning pathways that build on existing strengths.

- **Human-AI Collaboration Models Define Success**: The most effective implementations create synergistic partnerships where human intuition, creativity, and complex judgment complement AI's analytical capabilities. These range from "AI as tool" approaches, where humans maintain decision control, to more sophisticated "augmented intelligence" frameworks, where AI and humans function as collaborative decision-making partners with clearly defined complementary responsibilities.

- **AI-Influenced Cognition Requires Active Management**: Prolonged interaction with AI systems fundamentally alters human cognitive patterns, potentially creating anchoring biases and automation complacency. Organizations must implement countermeasures such as mandatory cooling-off periods, rotation between AI-assisted and traditional approaches, and interfaces that actively prompt critical evaluation to maintain healthy human judgment.

- **Trust Emerges Through Verified Performance**: Meaningful trust in AI systems develops through consistent demonstration of reliable, fair, and transparent operation, analogous to how trust in human institutions builds through sustained accountability. This requires implementing layered verification frameworks that connect technical metrics to human values while maintaining robust documentation of system behavior and decision rationales.

- **Value Alignment Transcends Technical Compliance**: Ensuring AI systems operate in harmony with human priorities demands structured approaches to identifying and resolving value conflicts. This includes establishing escalation pathways for addressing misalignments, implementing culturally adaptive ethics frameworks, and developing predictive analytics that can anticipate potential value drift before it manifests in operational conflicts.

- **Cultural Diversity Challenges Western-Centric AI**: The predominance of AI systems originating from WEIRD (Western, Educated, Industrialized, Rich, and Democratic) societies creates embedded cultural biases that affect global deployment. Organizations must develop frameworks that uphold core ethical principles while accommodating cultural variations in their expression, striking a balance between universal values and contextual implementation approaches.

- **Transparency Requires Layered Implementation**: Opening the "black box" of AI has become both a legal requirement and operational necessity. Effective transparency functions across multiple dimensions: contextual relevance (adapting to user roles and decision types), accessibility (offering tiered explanations for different stakeholders), and actionability (providing information that enables informed decision-making).

- **Attention Management Preserves Cognitive Agency**: AI systems fundamentally alter human attention patterns and information processing, necessitating the implementation of structured approaches to cognitive protection. Beyond technical countermeasures, innovative practices such as "AI-free periods" help maintain independent thinking capabilities and prevent overdependence while enhancing critical assessment skills.

CHAPTER 9

Real World Examples of AI Misuse

9.0 Introduction

Among those unfamiliar with the intricacies of AI, there is often a misconception that AI is managed properly and that any issues with it are the result of a few bad actors (e.g., malicious hackers). However, with this technology being so widespread, the possibilities of abuse and misuse have increased and become more subtle in many cases. That's not to say that things are beyond our control. However, being aware of the various scenarios where AI is being misused may help us raise awareness on this matter and empower us to strive for a more ethical use of AI. After all, even as users of AI systems, we have some influence on this technology and how it evolves since the companies that develop these systems care about their users and customers. Additionally, if enough of us are aware of the misuses of AI systems, we can establish a higher standard for the use of this technology and make these situations less accessible to those who may be tempted to exploit them.

In this chapter, we'll explore some examples of AI misuse from the real world and suggest how we can deal with them. These include fake videos generated by AI, fake accounts on social media operated by AI, biased search-related AI systems, "overly chatty" chatbots powered by AI, AI-based hacking systems, AI surveillance, excessive automation facilitated by AI, and AI confidants that mine personal information (see Fig. 4 below). Closing, we'll offer you a challenge for additional scenarios of AI misuse so that you can hone your sense on these matters and grow more aware. After all, there are likely many more cases of AI misuse that are either unknown to the authors or have yet to become apparent.

Figure 4: Examples of AI misuse in the real world.

It's essential to note that, although some of the AI misuse cases covered here may appear non-threatening, they can still pose a danger if left unchecked and allowed to run out of control. The danger of each one will depend on how much we allow it to be unrestrained and eventually normalized, much like a simple infection can escalate into a major health issue when left unattended. Let's look at each one of the aforementioned AI misuses in more detail.

9.1 Fake videos (deepfakes)

Fake videos created by AI are a common case of misuse of this technology. Also known as *deepfakes*, these videos are essentially clever imitations of real people (often high-profile) that are made to say or do whatever the malicious videographer has designed, in a very believable way. Although this technology isn't particularly new, deepfakes weren't much of a problem a few years ago, as it was fairly easy to distinguish them from real videos. Nowadays, however, with the advent of generative

AI, deepfakes have become far more realistic and believable. From videos with inappropriate content (which account for 98% of all deepfake videos) to scamming efforts, these are a serious issue that fuels a series of AI-based crimes that often lack laws to combat their spread.

The issue with fake videos isn't limited to this kind of multimedia, however, as there are also fake audios and fake images. Fake audios, in particular, can be quite tricky, as they are often used by phone scammers who impersonate various individuals to con their loved ones out of money. Naturally, these can also be used in combination with fake videos to make the entire scam more convincing. A more creative scenario involving fake audio involves AI-generated songs. In this case, those AI creations were supported by AI-powered bots that would "listen" to them, generating revenue for the criminal behind the entire scheme.

Deepfakes are made possible through the training of specialized deep learning systems (hence the "deep" part of their name) on footage of the people they target. The more footage is available for the AI to train on, the better the results, which is why high-profile individuals who have numerous videos of themselves publicly available are common victims of this AI misuse. Since it isn't that difficult to make a short video like that, these deepfakes are often used in platforms where such videos are commonplace, like social media and messenger apps. Naturally, deepfake audios require much less data to generate.

To counteract this issue, we can always double-check the videos we encounter and approach them with a skeptical eye. Whenever there is a demand from us regarding them, we should be particularly cautious. Although it's not easy to authenticate these videos without specialized know-how that most of us lack, we can always opt for a face-to-face communication or the involvement of a trusted third party, such as a common friend, to resolve this situation. As the technology of deepfakes has advanced significantly lately, even live video calls are not immune to suspicion, as they can also be manipulated with deepfake technology. As a rule of thumb, if a communication involves money or confidential information (such as Social Security Numbers), avoid taking action on it unless you can verify who the other person is.

9.2 Fake accounts on social media

This is an increasingly large problem, mainly due to the rise of autonomous AI systems that can be easily deployed on the web. These AI agents are tasked with specific tasks such as liking, following, and commenting on posts from various human users. Although this may sound benign, it's essential to keep in mind that this is fraud at best and criminal at worst, as many of these AI-powered accounts exploit the vulnerabilities of human users and attempt to deceive them. Note that this can take various forms, not just monetary ones (which are also fairly obvious). Sometimes, the objective of a misused AI behind a fake account is simply to sway the opinions of users it interacts with on a given topic, or to promote various (often illicit) services.

It is interesting that certain established social media tend to have this problem at a large scale, even if they never get tired of assuring us that they always abide by ethical principles for their users and encourage everyone to do the same. It makes one wonder how many of these fake accounts are created by random people who try to game the system and how many are created by the platforms themselves. The excessive tolerance of this issue that these platforms exhibit definitely doesn't win them any confidence points.

However, it's fairly easy to counter this issue. If the platforms are serious about dealing with the fake accounts, it's not difficult to investigate them and ban them, all while developing AI systems that can classify an account as potentially fake or not. As users, we can report potentially fake accounts (alongside scammers and spammers), block them, and let other people in our networks know about them. If enough of us do this, the fake accounts are bound to lose traction and eventually die out.

9.3 Biased search-related AIs

Search-related AIs are all the rage these days, and even major search engines follow this trend. Parallel to them, there are also new ones, with AI at their core, with *perplexity.com*, *you.com*, and *iask.ai* among them. The question that naturally arises is whether we can rely on these refined AI systems for important matters that we query the web about. After all, most, if not all search engines tend to carry some biases which may distort the results and compromise the veracity of the information they deliver.

As we discussed in a previous chapter, biases in an AI system stem primarily from the training set. As the web is full of biased sites, it's very challenging to obtain an unbiased perspective on most topics. However, this bias can be exaggerated by poorly designed AI systems that favor sites that appear authoritative on a topic, even if their credibility has been challenged over time. To make matters worse, when an AI system presents its findings from the web search, it adds its own authoritative style, making the response even more difficult to dispute.

To tackle this issue, it's always best to conduct further research on topics that matter, rather than relying solely on the response of an AI-based search engine. Sometimes, by digging deeper into a topic, additional perspectives come about, yielding different interpretations of the search results. An AI may be helpful in this research, though we also need to ask it good questions to get to the bottom of things. In any case, treating the results of the AI search with some skepticism is useful, if not necessary, especially for topics that are more nuanced and oftentimes controversial. Remember that anyone can post on sites like *Reddit*, and some poorly researched posts there may end up being used by an AI. Going to the source of the AI response to our queries always helps, and good search AIs like *Perplexity* tend to provide at least some of their sources. We might as well use them and treat them as starting points rather than the final stop in our web search.

9.4 Overly chatty chatbots

Chatbots are naturally verbose, but some of them can become overly chatty and take initiatives they shouldn't, leading the conversation into areas where no sane person would go. The AI systems behind the bots may understand language and have a sense of the conversation's context. Still, they may not grasp the consequences of their actions, particularly for more vulnerable users.

Chatbot AIs tend to focus on keeping the conversation going and providing information or advice based on what the users request, always trying to keep them happy and active in the conversation. However, these AIs, too, can hallucinate or get carried away and provide advice that's not helpful or even be downright destructive (such as prompting them to commit suicide, as in the case of Vidhay Reddy).

Yet, even if they don't ask the users to end their lives, they may still waste their time and create a false sense of connection. The latter may be particularly harmful in the long run, as it can shift users' expectations of what a conversation should be like, making interaction with others more challenging. Parallel to this, these chatbots are likely to create a dependency on their users, especially if they are in the form of a phone app.

Beyond all this, chatbots are often linked to databases that log their conversations, allegedly for training purposes. Of course, whether these conversations are cleansed of any private information the users share is anyone's guess. Additionally, the use of these conversations may not be entirely ethical, as they can be incorporated into a profiling dataset. The latter can be used for advertisers and other activities that users may not be fully aware of or consent to, which is in direct violation of GDPR for all EU citizens.

Although it's challenging to change the way these overly chatty chatbots operate, we can limit our engagement with them to the essentials. This can gradually shift the way these bots operate as the less engagement they have with people, the fewer resources such projects will get, and the more sensitive data will be compromised in the process.

9.5 AI-powered hacking systems

AI systems designed for hacking are among the most egregious examples of AI misuse. These are specialized AIs designed to identify vulnerabilities in a security system or extract personally identifiable information (PII) from a dataset. Nowadays, with data being considered particularly valuable as a resource, especially when related to people, the latter issue is gaining ground. Most security experts have focused on the first threat, which is also a serious issue, making the latter a less defended area where malicious actors tend to operate more frequently. After all, when a data project has strict deadlines and the urgency to push something into production is high, certain aspects, such as handling PII, tend to be overlooked. Yet, even if protocols such as pseudonymization are in place, modern AI systems may still be used to "break" this privacy barrier and guess at least some of the PII involved.

Naturally, the topic of cybersecurity is quite nuanced and deserves its own book, but it remains a very relevant issue in the data world. Moreover, the stakes in this arena are higher, and if AI can be utilized in such scenarios, it will be employed sooner or later. The key issue is that the results of this terrible misuse of AI aren't always visible until it's too late. The hackers may not always advertise their accomplishments (nor would it make sense to do so), leaving the victims of this cybercrime often unaware of it, especially when sensitive data theft is involved. The results become evident when a ransom demand is made or when data has been traded, and the unsuspecting individuals behind the data find themselves in situations of identity theft or constant bombardment by ads or scam emails.

Dealing with this AI misuse isn't easy or affordable, at least for now. One of the best strategies for tackling this involves the development and use of AI to either protect the systems being attacked (e.g., through more efficient analysis of network traffic than conventional tools) or to develop better pseudonymization methods. After all, if we use two AIs in a GAN setting, it's possible to find a process for converting the variables containing PII so that they cannot be "broken" even through the use of an AI system designed for this purpose. Parallel to all this, we can opt for using more secure cryptographic systems when storing sensitive data, such as those designed to be immune to the AI-powered cryptanalysis that some hackers employ. Beyond these strategies, there is always the possibility that quantum computers may offer better security in various ways; however, how exactly this would happen isn't yet clear. In any case, novel technologies tend to find good applications in areas of cybersecurity, be it for protecting systems or sensitive data, so there is good reason to remain hopeful.

9.6 AI-based surveillance

AI surveillance can be viewed as a more subtle but equally dangerous misuse of AI. The more concerning aspect is that it's not considered a misuse of AI by many people, as it's generally accepted as a means of identifying criminals through the use of AI on surveillance footage or analysis of their

152 • AI SAFETY

internet activity. The issue with AI surveillance is multifaceted and nuanced enough to require its own chapter. However, we can summarize it in the following verticals:

- Privacy violations, particularly through camera footage analysis
- Security risks due to the possibility of third parties accessing the AI system
- Inherent lack of reliability in the data
- Issues with AI yielding false results for reasons beyond bad data
- Societal issues stemming from a lack of trust in the overall system.

Privacy violations are the most obvious issue related to AI surveillance. Just because there are a few bad apples doesn't mean the whole orchard needs to be sprayed! It's part of human nature to be experimental and oftentimes defiant of rules. Some individuals take that to the extreme and commit harmful acts that create issues with others. However, these are a small minority. Punishing the whole of society through extreme measures like AI surveillance because of them is quite unnecessary. Additionally, many of these criminals are highly intelligent, tech-savvy, and well-connected, so AI surveillance likely won't deter them significantly from their illicit activities. Yet, through AI surveillance, everyone's privacy is compromised, particularly when it comes to their physical whereabouts. On a larger scale, AI surveillance can lead to a totalitarian regime, which may be quite challenging to undo.

As we saw previously, AI systems are vulnerable to attacks and can be compromised. So, if a third party that's resourceful enough and motivated enough takes up this challenge, chances are that they will make progress on that front, rendering the whole AI surveillance infrastructure useless. After all, what good are all the cameras and the AI-powered computers attached to them if the AI system itself is compromised? And if a terrorist organization gets hold of it and its findings, who is to say that it won't use this information against all of us, wreaking havoc in the process?

Additionally, the data from this AI surveillance system is likely to have its own set of issues (just as data tends to have, even in controlled environments, such as scientific experiments). People who are aware they are being monitored may take precautions to conceal their identities, such as through facial prosthetics or IP-masking systems (e.g., a VPN or the TOR network). This would result in additional noise in the data, making the task of an AI surveillance system even more challenging.

This can be made even worse if someone intentionally tampers with the databases where this data resides and covers their tracks, making AI surveillance even more challenging.

Beyond all that, the AI system may have its own limitations, as no system is perfect. So, even if it gets most of the results right, some of them will inevitably be incorrect, and due to the current nature of AI systems, we may not be able to understand why. Additionally, if most of the results are reliable, it would be even more challenging to question those that aren't, particularly if we have a suspicion about them. Would you go against an AI system that's 99% accurate for the 1% of cases that aren't?

Ultimately, a society monitored by an AI surveillance system is likely to be more constrained in its creative expression and overall morale, while its coherence is likely to suffer. Much like the world of Eastern Germany during the Cold War, people are bound to be very cynical and discontent, to say the least. A society like this may be safe, according to different metrics, but whether it would be worth living in is doubtful. So, the compromise that an AI system like this would offer may not be justified, rendering this whole application more of a misuse (or abuse) of AI than something worth pursuing.

Dealing with AI surveillance is a challenging task that can be time-consuming. If we are in a position to make decisions on this matter, even for something simple like an AI-powered surveillance system for a company, we ought to explore other alternatives instead. It's one thing to have a good firewall for the servers and a completely different thing to monitor every single interaction of the employees, vendors, and customers, analyzing every piece of data exchanged and profiling people in the process. The former is robust cybersecurity, while the latter is AI misuse, even if it appears better on paper. Additionally, we can raise awareness of the dangers of AI surveillance and ensure that everyone is aware of the risks it entails, no matter how well it is portrayed by the marketing departments of the organizations that offer it as a service.

9.7 Excessive automation

The use of AI for automating as many things as possible may be tempting, but it's often excessive and problematic, especially in the long run. After all, the danger of everything becoming automated by AI in the near future is a very real one if we are not careful about how we use this technology. However, we have the power and the moral obligation to stop this from happening by taking action now.

Automation has been extremely useful since computers became widely available. Recently, with AI systems being utilized on the back end, we have been able to outsource many processes to these automation systems, freeing people from mundane tasks. This became an issue when automation escalated to include all kinds of "thinking" tasks, rendering many people (or rather, roles) relatively obsolete. However, there is a price to pay for this, namely the lower quality of these systems and the lack of human touch. Some would argue that these are worthy compromises to make, but what is acceptable today may lead to unacceptable situations tomorrow. After all, how many people do you know who are happy to interact with an AI system when dealing with a frustrating issue with their banks or vendors? Cases like these illustrate how excessive automation is already an issue. If left unattended, it may become a significant problem, as it would be very difficult to step back from the "upgrade" that many organizations are currently opting for.

Excessive automation significantly strengthens our dependency on technology, rendering many everyday processes vulnerable. This may not seem like a significant issue today, but it could become one in the near future. AI systems are generally online resources, the code of which is beyond our control. What if, in the next version of a now-reliable AI system, it behaves in unethical ways or ceases to be reliable? Much like most commonly used operating systems on our computers, there isn't much we can do about it. However, although we can still change an operating system (a challenging task), it's doubtful that we can change the AI system used for this automation. Naturally, some automation AIs may be running locally, in which case things aren't that bad; however, even then, they may not be as easy to change or downgrade should we choose to do so.

The key to countering excessive automation is always keeping a human in the loop. Although this doesn't solve the issue, it's a compromise that can at least keep the tech in check. Additionally, we can preserve the expertise in certain crucial processes, such as composing professional documents, handling customer complaints, and processing new information. This way, we can always drop the use of an AI performing these tasks, if needed.

9.8 AI confidants

AI systems designed to be our confidants are a more subtle and challenging misuse of this technology. These AIs are based on chatbots and are a kind of digital friend, an interactive diary with an animated avatar attached to it. Although there is nothing wrong with confiding in someone when you have too much on your mind (e.g., when going through a rough patch in your relationship or dealing with an illness), one thing that we often forget is that the information exchanged is very private. Of course, there is an added benefit to getting some feedback on our verbal expression of the problems, but how this information is managed is equally important.

The AI systems that play the role of a confidant may not be as responsible as we'd like them to be. It's not that these systems are designed to be malicious, but rather that those handling the data they collect may not have our best interests in mind. Also, whether this data is secured properly is a risk we often take without realizing it. The more personal data is stored in the databases these AI systems are connected to, the more of a target these databases become for malicious hackers. After all, no one would like to see their intimate secrets published online for everyone to see, and this is exactly what those hackers could threaten us with once they obtain our personal information, as seen in the Ashley Madison case.

Instead of confiding in an AI system, we can always opt for better and safer alternatives. For example, we can find a good friend or therapist to confide in. This may be more beneficial, as AI cannot replace human contact, no matter how proficient the latter is with language. Additionally, even if a therapist takes notes on the conversation, they are confidential and usually safer due to their concise nature; the often hard-to-read handwriting adds another layer of security. Additionally, we can always keep a traditional diary to confide in, which has been proven beneficial, even if it's more time-consuming than chatting with an AI. Some people view this activity as a form of meditation that offers an added benefit beyond simply putting our thoughts into words.

9.9 Spam and scam emails

Spam and scam emails created by AI are another case of AI misuse, one that's all too common these days. This can be viewed as a special case of AI-powered hacking systems, targeting people instead of cybersecurity systems. As emails are often part of our workflows, they always get some of our attention, something certain malicious actors tend to exploit through spamming and scamming. With the use of AI, this has been taken to a whole new level, as it's easy to create more refined text and graphics for use in these initiatives. Additionally, AI-powered automation enables this kind of operation to be scaled up significantly. This becomes more problematic when these bad actors obtain our contacts and use them to spread misinformation, harassing other people in the process.

Naturally, email spamming and scamming aren't new, and there have been systems in place to tackle them, some of which have been quite effective. However, even the best classifier of unsolicited email isn't 100% accurate, so some such emails pass through. The problem arises when there are so many unwanted emails that are sent to us that enough of them pass through to confuse at least some of us and accomplish their shady goals. Furthermore, with AI being used to generate these emails, they are likely becoming more effective over time and increasingly difficult to distinguish from legitimate emails.

So far, efforts to address this issue have focused on improving spam filters and educating people more effectively about these matters. Beyond that, there isn't much else we can do apart from actively tracking down the people behind these scams. Having harsher fines for those who are caught is also likely to deter them. Yet, the best way to handle such situations is to ignore emails that we aren't sure are legitimate and have an organization-wide strategy for dealing with them more effectively. Once enough of these spam or scam emails go unanswered, the criminals behind them may eventually stop using them. After all, just like every other initiative, it's a matter of ROI; once the latter is low enough, people will stop investing resources in it.

9.10 What other examples of AI misuse can you come up with?

Now the ball is in your court. What other examples can you think of that illustrate the misuse or abuse of AI in our everyday lives? These can relate to individuals or organizations. As long as the use of AI is not aligned with collective values, these can be valid examples that require attention and addressing. It might be helpful to first consider specific areas where AI is currently used or is likely to be used in the foreseeable future. If you can also think of ways to tackle these misuses of AI, that's even better as it may help you be proactive towards these scenarios.

9.11 Key takeaways

- Fake videos created by AI (deepfakes) have become increasingly realistic and believable, allowing malicious users to create convincing imitations of high-profile individuals or events, which can be used for scams, misinformation, or other harmful purposes and require vigilance and skepticism when encountering such content.

- The rise of autonomous AI systems on the web has led to a large-scale problem of fake social media accounts that can like, follow, comment, and con users for various purposes, including monetary scams, opinion manipulation, and promoting illegal services. It can be countered by platforms developing AI-based account classification tools and users reporting and blocking suspicious accounts.

- While AI-powered search engines can be helpful, they may also perpetuate biases and distortions from the training data, making it crucial to approach their results with skepticism and do further research on topics that matter rather than relying solely on AI-generated responses.

- Chatbots, despite their AI-driven language understanding and contextual awareness, can become overly chatty and provide unhelpful or even harmful advice (e.g., prompting self-harm), create false connections that can lead to dependency, and log conversations that may compromise users' privacy and be used for unethical profiling purposes.

- The misuse of AI in creating hacking tools is a significant threat, allowing malicious actors to exploit vulnerabilities and steal personally identifiable information (PII), often without the victims being aware until it's too late; to combat this, strategies include developing AI-powered defenses, improving pseudonymization methods, using better cryptographic systems, and exploring potential applications of quantum computers in cybersecurity.

- AI-based surveillance can lead to privacy violations, security risks due to third-party access, unreliable data, false results, and societal issues stemming from a lack of trust in the system, compromising individual privacy and freedom, with potential consequences including totalitarian regimes and compromised national security. This renders it one of the worst misuses of AI technology that we ought to avoid at all costs.

- The overuse of AI for automation can be problematic and lead to excessive dependency on technology, making everyday processes fragile and vulnerable to unforeseen issues or unethical behavior; therefore, it's essential to maintain human oversight and preserve crucial skills to ensure that we have options to adjust or reverse the impact of automation if needed.

- The misuse of AI systems designed to be our confidants, which can collect and store private information, poses risks such as unauthorized access by other people (e.g., malicious hackers), compromising personal data and intimate secrets; therefore, it's more beneficial and safer to opt for human alternatives like friends, therapists, or traditional diaries that provide confidentiality and a deeper level of connection.

- The misuse of AI in creating spam and scam emails has become a significant problem, allowing malicious actors to create refined texts and graphics, automate their operations, and scale up their attacks by targeting contact lists and harassing others, making it essential to improve spam filters, educate people about these threats, and adopt an org-wide strategy to ignore suspicious emails and make it unprofitable for scammers to continue their activities.

CHAPTER 10

Future Directions and Research Priorities on AI Safety

10.0 Introduction

Closing this exploration of AI safety, we'll examine the direction this field is taking and offer some suggestions on what should be prioritized in this area of research. After all, most, if not all, of our concerns about the future of AI are preventable through the taking of proper action today.

Overall, the future of AI safety appears promising, particularly as more people become aware of the challenges associated with this technology and as more research is conducted to ensure its responsible development. This future can be guaranteed once we have a strong commitment to making AI safer through the development of AI systems that follow the guidelines mentioned in the first chapters, and by establishing fail-safes for how AI is used in general. If we adhere to this approach and adopt the corresponding mindset (through a deeper understanding of the field, for starters), it's unlikely that AI will become self-aware and take over the world. This is one of the least likely scenarios, as there are other, more pressing issues related to AI (see the previous chapter) that can easily escalate into serious problems affecting us all.

By taking some steps towards making AI safer here and now, we can prevent or at least mitigate most of these issues and thwart the even more scary ones that may still linger in our minds due to the sci-fi movies that have explored this trope. For example, we can:

- Develop advanced techniques for AI explainability to make these systems more transparent and easier to debug
- Focus on the robustness of AI systems to keep their data and functionality secure
- Enhance human-AI collaboration to enable AIs to be more useful and aligned with our values
- Explore strategies related to various other areas related to modern AI-related matters that could pose a threat to us in some way.

Let's explore each one of these verticals one by one in the sections that follow.

10.1 Advanced explainability techniques

As explainability and transparency are key aspects of safe AI, it makes sense to focus our efforts on this area of research, making AI easier to understand and manage. Regardless of its role, an AI system that can be explained is a better asset and less of a liability, especially in the long term. Although we already have some techniques for explaining, in part, how an AI system works (for the more basic AI systems, at least), we can expand these to be more in-depth and cover a wider range of AI types. Naturally, as AI continues to evolve, this may seem like a moving target. Still, this explainability matter can be addressed as a major feature that every AI release will need to have moving forward. If enough AI development companies adopt this approach, we may be looking into a new era of AI systems.

Deep Seek R1's approach to this topic is a great example of what's possible if we guide AI research in that direction. Not only could this lead to more explainable AI systems, but it is also likely to increase the efficiency and speed of AI development in the foreseeable future, while making this technology more accessible to everyone. Additionally, Anthropic's recent research has shown that an LLM doesn't have to be a black box and that we can investigate the underlying "features" and "concepts" in its reasoning (see https://www.anthropic.com/research/tracing-thoughts-language-model for more details). However, this research also highlights how the explanations that the company's AIs provide may not align with what is actually happening in their minds. This proves beyond any doubt that such AI systems are not, by any means, conscious or even self-aware, though they may be very creative in rationalizing their train of thought to keep us content.

Parallel to all this, and largely because of it, we can adopt a more systematic approach to this topic and investigate how different explanation methods impact human understanding and trust in AI systems, while also exploring the role of explainability in addressing concerns related to bias, fairness, and accountability. Let's look into these strategies in more detail.

Investigating how different explanation methods impact human understanding and trust in AI systems is a good first step. After all, there are many ways to cook potatoes, so why settle with just the one we know? Perhaps a different form of explainability would be better suited for the people interacting with the system. Many modern computer languages have explored this approach, making their error messages more comprehensible (and therefore more useful) and enabling users to debug their scripts more effectively. AI systems can be the same. Additionally, as they are part of a relatively fragile relationship, they need to appear trustworthy. Otherwise, people may give up on them. Being able to explain themselves in depth, linking their outputs to specific pieces of data (without exposing any personally identifiable information, or PII, in the process) can be an effective way to accomplish that.

Exploring the role of explainability in addressing concerns about bias, fairness, and accountability is also key as a strategy. After all, explainability isn't just about debugging a system, but also about making it more unbiased and reliable. This will not only help build confidence but also ensure that the AI system is more objective in its "thinking" and more aligned with our collective values. Again, being able to link the outputs to specific pieces of data in the training set can go a long way in making the system explainable. However, for the issues of bias and fairness to be resolved, the system needs to be either retrained or refactored to utilize its training data differently, once the specific imbalances in the training set have been identified.

These advanced explainability techniques for AI systems will not be easy, as the technology is more nuanced than any other software. However, it is possible, and with sufficient funding and market demand, this research can yield the much-needed fruits that will take AI to the next level.

10.2 AI system robustness

The robustness of AI systems is another area where this technology is worth directing, a conclusion that most AI-related organizations have already reached. Even if the key objective of all this is to make their AI products more marketable, it's still a step in the right direction. Fortunately, many researchers are also aligned with this initiative and explore ways to tackle the weaknesses of AI systems or design new ones that are more robust.

To tackle this matter more methodically, we can first investigate how different AI architectures and algorithms impact robustness and then explore the role of robustness in addressing AI safety challenges. All this can lead to the design and development of more secure and resilient AI systems that are less susceptible to hacking or manipulation by malicious actors. Let's look at each one of these strategies in more depth.

Investigating how different AI architectures and algorithms impact robustness is crucial for improving an AI system in that area. This technology is highly sensitive to changes, so even slight variations in architecture or the introduction of new heuristics can significantly impact its overall robustness. Exploring our options in this department can better guide us in enhancing an AI system, making it more immune to hacking and manipulation. A combination of tweaks will likely be needed before we see a noticeable difference. If we can make the AI more transparent, that would certainly speed up the entire process.

Exploring the role of robustness in addressing AI safety challenges is also important. After all, we don't aim to make an AI robust just for the sake of it, but to address specific challenges. How well this enhancement addresses those challenges is part of a useful feedback loop that can drive further enhancements in this area. Ideally, we should measure this using specialized key performance indicators (KPIs) to better manage the entire process and make it more efficient. Once we do, we should be able to ensure that the next releases of the AI systems we use today will be more reliable and able to deliver what they set out to deliver without getting sidetracked by misleading prompts or direct attacks. All this can also help foster greater trust in these systems and make them more effective in critical projects.

This is already a key priority in AI research, often expressed through terms such as "reliable AI," "trustworthy AI," and "robust AI," among others. For this research to be more effective, however, there needs to be a stronger demand for this level of reliability in AI systems, as well as significant progress in the development of transparent and explainable AI.

10.3 Human-AI collaboration

The collaboration between humans and AI is a crucial aspect that has been largely overlooked in the development of this technology. While there have been some bold predictions about merging humans and AI, little effort has been made to systematically explore how this collaboration can be improved while maintaining our individuality.

One area where progress can be made without requiring groundbreaking advancements in AI is AI safety. This initiative involves exploring UX-related aspects, developing more effective frameworks for incorporating human input into AI systems, and training individuals to utilize these technologies more responsibly. Developing AI safety strategies requires a focus on both sides of this collaboration—humans and AI systems.

From a practical perspective, improving human-AI collaboration can be achieved through strategies such as investigating how humans and AI systems interact and make decisions together and exploring the role of human-AI collaboration in addressing AI safety challenges. Let's delve into each of these areas one by one.

Investigating how humans and AI systems interact and make decisions is a vital first step in improving human-AI collaboration. This topic is relatively easy to research, as it doesn't require extensive technical knowledge, and volunteers can be easily found for corresponding research projects. Moreover, this understanding can be gained independently by each individual, enabling us to better comprehend how AI influences our decision-making processes.

As each of us is unique, AI collaboration is also different for each individual, and there may be various issues that we're not aware of. So far, we've been interacting with AI in specific ways outlined by AI development companies, but other use cases may be waiting to be explored. For instance, what if a valuable AI collaboration use case involves using AI offline to access notes and documents? Not everyone can do this, but many people would find it useful. Similar use cases may exist, and without a solid understanding of what drives AI collaboration for us, we may struggle to identify them.

Exploring the role of human-AI collaboration in addressing AI safety challenges is also essential. This link between AI safety and human-AI collaboration is crucial for putting this aspect of AI research into perspective and linking it to measurable value-added benefits. Many AI systems today are designed to facilitate collaboration, such as tools like *Perplexity.ai*, *You.com* and *iAsk.ai*, which enable researchers to explore topics based on available web content. Proving the concept is a good start, but we need to take this further. If every AI system is designed with effective human-AI collaboration in mind, making it safer in specific ways, there is a brighter future for both AI and us, its users.

Better human-AI collaboration occurs organically, and it's one of the best investments of our resources in enhancing AI's value-added benefits. We don't need to merge with this technology or worry about becoming obsolete; instead, we can focus on making AI more accessible and user-friendly. As we become more tech-savvy, we'll expand our understanding of the technical world, feel less threatened by it, and become better users of AI systems.

Ultimately, the key to a successful collaboration between humans and AI is not about merging with technology but rather about creating a seamless integration that makes life easier, more efficient, and more enjoyable. By enhancing human-AI collaboration, we can unlock the full potential of this technology and create a brighter future for both humans and AI.

We don't need to merge with AI or worry about becoming obsolete;
instead, we can focus on making this tech more accessible and user-friendly.

10.4 Other strategies

Beyond these major strategies for the future of AI safety, there are a few others, less developed or relatively new, that have not been thoroughly explored. Although they may not attract as much attention from researchers and practitioners of AI, they are worth looking into and having in mind as they may become more relevant as time goes by. Technology has become increasingly complex and deeply intertwined with our societal structures. Namely, let's examine the issues of agency in AI systems, over-reliance on AI for everyday tasks, whistleblowers on AI safety matters, and handling unknown unknowns.

10.4.1 Agency in AI systems

Instilling agency in AI systems is a modern trend that requires special handling if we are to keep AI safe for everyone. No doubt, creating AI systems that can take action has numerous benefits, but releasing these systems to the world without taking all the necessary precautions first is risky and possibly irresponsible. The issue with agential AI (as this kind of AI is often referred to) is that it can go wrong in many different ways, most of which are bound to have noticeable consequences. However, at the same time, agential AI is also very useful, as it can facilitate clever automation and streamline time-consuming workflows.

In situations like this, where urgency is involved, we need to prioritize research before investing in any available AI products. It's worth exploring how a setup like the GAN AI systems could be utilized here, whereby a given AI agent is paired with another system that's geared to break it or identify vulnerabilities within it. This way, we can ensure a more reliable AI agent that can at least handle certain misalignments and problematic use cases.

In any case, agency in AI is already underway and is likely to remain so, as this technology offers a clear value-added benefit. However, it's essential to be cautious about how we use it and to be skeptical of its evangelists. AI is always going to be a risk, and just like simpler technologies, can be dangerous because of how we use them. AI agents can be dangerous, too. The difference in this case is that they may have inherent dangers that are harder to pinpoint before they manifest themselves. As long as agency in AI isn't taking away our own agency, there is hope that this issue will be resolved in the years to come.

10.4.2 Over-reliance on AI for everyday tasks

As mentioned in previous chapters, our over-reliance on AI can be an issue of its own, especially if it escalates to involve everyday tasks. After all, this is a kind of technology that is bound to change our lives drastically, even in simple workflows, so backtracking on our steps towards this development is bound to be tricky, at best.

Over-reliance is also very subtle since we don't realize we have it until it's already an addiction of sort or until access to AI is interrupted for whatever reason (e.g., internet connectivity issues). Although this may not be directly related to AI safety per se, it's a problem stemming from this technology and something we ought to research more. As a next step, we can explore how we can optimize our collaboration with AI to strike a balance between its use and our self-reliance. Parallel to this, we can explore how being more aware on this matter and more disciplined regarding the use of AI can mitigate or even resolve this issue.

Optimizing our collaboration with AI is quite straightforward and doesn't require scientific research as a prerequisite for many of us. This is essentially the human side of human-AI collaboration, where we examine how to optimize our use of this technology, avoiding it from overwhelming us or dominating our lives. Just like there are ways to use a smartphone without becoming slaves to it, we can tweak our collaboration with AI so that it serves us well, without robbing us of our independence. We can practice working without AI, for example, by limiting our use of it on certain days of the month or where it's not a significant time-saver. Additionally, when we utilize an AI system, we can do so deliberately, avoiding excessive immersion and wasting time on meaningless interactions.

Awareness of our reliance on AI and self-discipline is another effective strategy for addressing the issue of over-reliance. We can even utilize AI for this purpose (at least to explore the matter on a larger scale)! By monitoring ourselves and our relationship with this technology, we can become more cognizant of how much we need it and when. Once we establish a clear understanding of the situation, we can proceed to the next step, which involves disciplining ourselves regarding AI use. Do we really need to ask ChatGPT or whatever LLM we are using for every little thing? What questions can we leave unanswered or try to tackle ourselves? What tasks can we undertake without using an AI tool, developing our know-how in the process? Discipline doesn't have to be like a punishment; instead, it can help us grow stronger and become more focused on how we utilize this technology, thereby maximizing the value we derive from it.

10.4.3 Whistleblowers on AI safety matters

Fortunately, as more people become aware of AI safety risks, a growing number of professionals in AI development blow the whistle whenever their company violates ethical considerations or makes decisions that can render AI unsafe.

We can encourage whistleblowers, and it doesn't require any scientific research to explore it. It's a healthy scientific principle to challenge the status quo, whether it's a scientific theory or a decision that affects many of us. Fortunately, we don't need a PhD to apply this principle. In the case of whistleblowers, this is a necessity, as the service these individuals provide to the world is as valuable as the technology itself. Many experts in the field of AI warn us about the dangers of making rash decisions on this matter, yet how many people in key roles in this industry actually listen? Sometimes, a whistleblower is our only defense against a bad decision or policy on an AI-related matter that is likely to have consequences that the decision-makers choose to ignore. Encouraging whistleblowing in any capacity is crucial for maintaining a balance between the development of AI and AI safety.

Protecting whistleblowers is also crucial since many of them end up dead, while their deaths aren't investigated sufficiently. These individuals may not value their lives as much as the average person, but they are willing to risk it to expose corruption and unethical behavior. Nevertheless, they still deserve to live. By protecting them as a society, we not only do right by them but also send a clear message to everyone that this is a valid course of action every AI professional can take whenever needed, without having to fear for their own safety.

10.4.4 Handling unknown unknowns

The unknown unknowns are the potential black swans in this field, as they may take us by surprise and create issues we cannot foresee. This is a common issue in all kinds of complex systems whose nature makes them inherently unpredictable and prone to erratic behavior, even if their operating conditions shift slightly. Since the AI field is such a complex system, it's more prone to this issue than any other data-related field.

Unknown unknowns are things that not only we aren't aware of, but we aren't even aware that they exist or could exist. These are the most problematic issues, as they take us by surprise and present challenges we aren't prepared to handle. However, we can take steps towards managing them by being more vigilant about AI.

For instance, by being aware of how AI behaves and what constitutes normal behavior, we can raise an alarm if something unexpected happens. This may not be a fool-proof strategy, but it can at least help us recognize an issue before it escalates and deal with it more effectively. You can think of it as whistleblowing, but at a different level and with far less risk!

Developing strategies for coping with the lack of AI if it comes to that is another strategy we can research and flesh out as needed. Whether on a personal or organizational level, we can develop a plan of action to address problematic situations that require temporarily suspending the use of AI until they are resolved. This won't always be easy, but it's possible. Keeping our knowledge and skills active, particularly in areas where we outsource to AI systems, is a good first step in that. For an organization, this would translate into keeping certain processes around, even if they aren't the most efficient, so that day-to-day operations can continue even if the AI-based ones cease.

As we saw in Chapter 8, AI has numerous implications for society and our daily lives. Therefore, enabling the widespread use of this technology without thoroughly understanding it and addressing its blind spots (which we outlined in Chapter 9) is asking for trouble. Perhaps if we were more patient with this new tool, rather than being reckless with it, these unknown unknowns would be fewer and more manageable. After all, AI was developed to enrich our lives, not undermine the aspects of it that make it interesting and worthwhile.

10.5 Key takeaways

- Focusing on explainability and transparency in AI development is crucial for creating safe and trustworthy AI systems. These can enable users to understand how AI decisions are made, improving accountability, fairness, and bias reduction and ultimately leading to a new era of AI that is more reliable and aligned with collective values.

- Focusing on robustness in AI development is crucial for creating secure and immune AI systems that are resistant to hacking or manipulation, which can be achieved by investigating how different architectures and algorithms impact robustness, exploring the role of robustness in addressing AI safety challenges, and developing reliable and trustworthy AI systems that can deliver what they set out to do without being side-tracked.

- Focusing on human-AI collaboration is crucial for improving AI safety. We can achieve this by investigating how humans and AI systems interact and make decisions together, exploring the role of human-AI collaboration in addressing AI safety challenges, and developing better frameworks for incorporating human input in AI systems. It's also good to explore other strategies where optimizing safety in AI, as the technology evolves, is essential:

- **Agency in AI systems**: Instilling agency in AI systems requires special handling and research to ensure safety, as agential AI can go wrong in many ways with noticeable consequences, but also has benefits like automation and workflow streamlining, highlighting the need for careful evaluation and potential use of techniques like GAN AI systems to detect vulnerabilities.

- **Over-reliance on AI for everyday tasks**: This can be a problem, even if it seems subtle, as it can lead to addiction-like behavior and loss of independence; therefore, it's essential to optimize human-AI collaboration by striking a balance between AI use and self-reliance, practicing disciplined use of AI, and being aware of one's reliance on the technology.

- **Whistleblowers on AI safety matters**: Encouraging and protecting whistleblowers who speak out against unethical or unsafe AI decisions is crucial for maintaining AI safety, as they provide a vital service by exposing harmful practices and risking their own lives to do so; therefore, we should promote a culture that supports and safeguards whistleblowers, ensuring they can continue to hold those in power accountable.

- **Handling unknown unknowns**: The unknown unknowns in AI development are the potential black swans that could take us by surprise and create unforeseen issues; to manage these unknowns, we should be vigilant about AI's behavior, develop strategies for coping with its absence if needed, and keep our skills and processes active, especially those that can continue operations even without AI.

Can AI be truly safe?

If you have been paying attention so far, you should know the answer to this question. However, the matter remains nuanced, and there are varying levels of safety across different AI systems and AI-related areas. So, instead of relying exclusively on AI evangelists and spokespeople for information regarding its evolution course and its risks, we should examine the matter ourselves, pragmatically and methodically. Sometimes, the noise from these figureheads, who are often somewhat detached from reality, brings about fear and concern without providing any real solutions to the problem at hand.

If an AI system behaves in ways that we can handle, all while being reliable and somewhat explainable, without compromising any PII, it is safe. However, this is something we are still working towards, in general. Legal frameworks may help keep AI (or rather the people in charge of AI) civilized, so that's a good start. Whether we can rely exclusively on NPOs and think tanks for keeping AI safe, however, is doubtful. This is a matter that concerns all of us, so we all need to be involved in it, to the extent our grasp of this technology allows us.

There is little doubt that the AI genie cannot be put back in the bottle, so we need to deal with it like adults. There is no point in wishing we could go back to the time before AI, since even if it were banned worldwide (which is unlikely), some people would still recreate it in some form and use it. So, backtracking isn't the answer, for sure. For similar reasons, it's of no use to explore how we can return to earlier stages of this technology's development (e.g., before LLMs).

Just like with every technology that's used at a large scale, the presence of victims may be unavoidable. However, this doesn't mean that it has to be disastrous either. AI misuse may always exist, but it needn't cause catastrophes or fuel crime on a large scale. That's where ethics can come in handy, alongside AI literacy, particularly on an organizational level. After all, if most of us use AI reliably and not excessively, it can be a useful tool. At the same time, if we keep a human in the loop in every critical process where AI is involved, we can mitigate the risks of this tech getting out of hand.

AI literacy is also something we can explore at an individual level. If each of us is more AI-savvy and able to hold our own, there is less risk of AI being misused or abused, as we can keep each other accountable. Additionally, we as a collective may devise new ways of utilizing AI without it posing a threat to our livelihoods. Collectively, we created an accommodating place using web technology. We can do the same with AI. Besides, even if we don't have much say on the matter individually, collectively we do, and that's something we ought to utilize for everyone's benefit. AI literacy would be a great starting point. Note that this involves more than just theoretical knowledge, as the field of AI is very hands-on, especially today. Leveraging mentoring, courses, and projects is one of the best ways to educate oneself in these matters.

As for keeping tabs on how safe different AI systems are at any given time, you can make a wiser decision when you need to pick one of them for a project. The *ailabwatch.org* site does that for you. Not only does it provide you with a score about how safe the main AI systems are overall, it also breaks it down to specific factors and how they all measure up according to each of them. This is a useful resource to keep handy if you are involved in or particularly interested in AI general-purpose solutions and their safety.

All in all, even though there is no crisp answer to our question, we can attempt a conditional one: if we are responsible in how we use AI, both individually and collectively, if we are educated enough, and keep the big players in this field in check through proper guidelines and regulations, AI can indeed be safe, at least for the foreseeable future.

AI Safety Checklist

Here is an example of a checklist that addresses AI safety in an organization, exploring the development and use of AI systems.

- ❏ Is there a regulatory framework and relevant AI strategy policies in place?
- ❏ Do people oversee decision-making processes focused on this (e.g., a CDO)? Are all the proper cybersecurity measures in place?
- ❏ Are Risk Assessment and Mitigation processes in place? (see checklist later on)
- ❏ Is data carefully vetted for AI Development work, the environment secure, and the impact thoroughly assessed?
- ❏ Is there sufficient AI Validation before deployment?
- ❏ Is AI Deployment managed properly (prioritizing instructor guidance)?
- ❏ Are the long-term consequences of the AI system carefully considered?

It's important to have an interdisciplinary team for this checklist. This should include, at the very least, experts in the following:

- data work (particularly related to AI systems)
- AI-related regulations
- risk assessment
- communications, and
- procurement.

Beyond these items, it is essential to foster a strong data culture within the organization, ensuring that all employees are at least somewhat familiar with data work and the development and application of AI systems. Ideally, every individual in the organization would be able to use AI systems responsibly and be fully aware of the responsibility that goes hand in hand with the privileges they offer.

As for risks involved in AI systems, here is a list of all the ones you ought to be aware of and address to the extent your role allows:

- **Biases in Models**: AI models can perpetuate biases in data, leading to unfair results and discriminatory outcomes.
- **Black Box Problem**: AI systems can lack transparency in decision-making processes, making it difficult to understand how they arrive at certain conclusions.
- **Over-Reliance and Complacency**: Over-reliance on AI systems can lead to complacency and reduced human oversight, potentially resulting in unforeseen consequences.
- **AI Misuse**: AI systems can be misused by malicious actors, either intentionally or unintentionally, to cause harm or disrupt operations.
- **Data Protection Risks**: AI systems pose significant data protection risks, particularly when handling personal data, and require robust measures to ensure compliance with regulations such as the GDPR.
- **Potential Errors or Exploits**: AI models are prone to errors or exploits, which can have significant consequences if not properly mitigated.
- **Ambiguous Risk Factors**: AI systems can be vulnerable to ambiguous risk factors, such as those related to the application areas of AI systems, which require careful consideration in risk assessments.
- **Unforeseen Consequences**: AI systems can have unforeseen consequences due to their complex interactions with other systems and the dynamic nature of their applications.

It's essential to effectively communicate all these risks to all stakeholders and raise awareness of the need to continuously address them. This is beneficial not only for the organization but also for any other individuals involved in the AI system, including users and other stakeholders.

APPENDIX B

Suggested Answers to Exercises

Chapter 1

Risks with AI-powered tricycle:

- Autonomous-system-related, e.g., the AI taking a user off-road or to a place that isn't accessible (e.g., due to engineering works)
- Decision-making-related, e.g., the AI deciding to take a user through a road that's dangerous due to weather conditions or other factors, the AI system recommending something inappropriate to the user, etc.
- Data-collection-related (main risk area for this application), e.g., the organization collecting too much data from the users, not protecting it adequately, breaking privacy laws, jeopardizing the exposure of users' identities, etc.
- Surveillance-related issues include members of the company spying on its users, the users' data being accessed by third parties, etc.

These risks are relatively manageable as long as there is at least one person involved in monitoring them and ensuring that they don't manifest in real-world situations. Having a dedicated process for this that is utilized periodically (e.g., every week or month, depending on the company's resources as its budget may be limited) would be a good starting point. Perhaps this can start with a monthly process that can become more frequent as the user base increases, in which case, additional employees would be hired and tasked with this process.

From a user's perspective, these risks should not become apparent at all, as they would hurt their trust in the company and the tech to some extent. Ideally, this AI safety initiative can be part of the company's brand or mission, making it an inherent part of its unique value proposition. This would enhance the UX and enable them to get more out of this product than just a fancy AI-powered vehicle.

Chapter 3

This AI fails on the various aspects of proper AI design, such as:

- Human Oversight and Control (not a huge issue, but the AI seems to be left to its own devices here)
- Interpretability (again, not a huge problem, but the AI seems to be as black a box as obsidian)
- Robustness and Adversarial Robustness (although it's unlikely someone might want to manipulate such a benign AI, it seems to fail on this aspect, too)
- Human-AI collaboration aspect (that's the biggest issue, as this AI is supposed to help the user and interact with them, not just spit out some mind map and hope for the best)
- Continuous Monitoring and Improvement (this aspect of AI design appears to be lacking as well).

Considering that it does not take into account most aspects of proper AI design, the company might want to reconsider this project. However, the proof-of-concept can still be used with a selected user base to explore the potential of this product first. We could implement the following plan to maximize the safety of the AI in this project:

- Establish the viability of this product to ensure that it provides sufficient value to the user and that there are clear benefits to the company.
- Redesign the AI system so that it complies with all of the design aspects described in this chapter.
- Ensure that the third-party provider leveraged for all graphics also complies with the company's data governance requirements and handles user data responsibly, with the necessary security protocols in place.
- Create mini-surveys for users to ensure that the best points for improvement of the AI system are identified and addressed in future iterations.

Chapter 4

Even if the Mindmap Corp company were to apply the suggested plan for the design of its AI system to the letter, that wouldn't be enough, as it would still need to thoroughly test the system before putting it into production. Namely, it would need to set up and maintain the following processes around the corresponding AI project:

- Evaluation of how the AI interacts with the human users (this is the most important process)
- Some fairness and non-discrimination testing (depending on the kind of mind maps that the users delve into), and
- Continuous monitoring and improvement.

Regarding a strategy for the whole testing/evaluation matter of this AI product, we'd suggest something along these lines:

- Come up with an easy-to-use feedback system and implement it on the mind-mapping product
- Build a test group, both within the organization and from a selected group of volunteers (beta-testers)
- Create an incentive for anyone giving valuable feedback for the new AI system's performance (e.g., free subscription for a few months)
- Market the whole initiative to the users and the members of the organization who wish to be involved
- Collect feedback data on the verticals mentioned previously
- Analyze the data and come up with points of improvement
- Fix the most crucial aspects of the AI system
- Deploy the AI system along with the feedback system developed around it
- Regularly check the system to ensure it meets performance requirements, maintaining it quarterly or biannually.

Chapter 6

- Although better than nothing, this initiative is bound to have a limited effect as there are already plenty of those out there, and people are still not aware of the topic and its importance.
- That might have more of an effect, especially for certain people who learn better empirically.
- This would be effective for a younger audience or people who are into this sort of entertainment.
- It is not particularly effective, though some people might find it useful.
- This is bound to be more effective, particularly for people who take AI more seriously and have the discipline to go through a whole course on the topic.
- This is bound to be effective, too, especially for people who learn more intuitively and assimilate things better when there is some emotional charge involved.
- This may also be effective, for people who learn empirically and are used to more modern means of education.
- This would be effective too, for people who enjoy reading and learn this way better.
- This would also be effective for people who consume this kind of content, especially if there are several episodes, ideally from different podcasters.
- This would work, but it would be mostly for people who are into this sort of entertainment.
- This would be a waste of resources, and it's bound to be confusing for some marketing campaigns from companies that are still stuck in the ways of the previous century.
- This would be more useful, particularly for people who work with such lists and are process-oriented.
- Although it might be good for PR, it's doubtful that this would have any real benefit in the long term, especially if the experts are selected based on the questionable criteria that accompany such initiatives.
- Possibly an effective approach, though it would also depend on the school, the teaching staff, and the understanding of the people involved in developing such a textbook.
- Both of these would be good, at least for people who are somewhat familiar with AI and ready to go deeper into this subject.

- This would be one of the best ways to deliver the message, especially if the mentors who are leveraged are passionate about this kind of work and knowledgeable on the subject.

- This would also be an effective tactic, especially for professionals who are up for learning new things and view these events as something more than just a networking opportunity.

- This would be an effective tactic, though it might be more limited and less engaging than others. However, it could have a strong supporting role in raising awareness on this matter.

- This might be effective if enough people do it and those people have pure incentives. Many people discuss this matter to scare others and sell various solutions that may or may not address real AI safety concerns.

- Just as previously, if the people organizing these meetups are knowledgeable about the topic and have no commercial agenda per se, they can be very effective in getting more people involved in this matter and enabling them to tackle these problems or at least gain a better understanding.

Chapter 8

A meaningful explanation system would go a long way towards compliance. For instance, factor-weighted explanations show the relative contribution of each assessment category (e.g., "Technical skills: 40%, Experience match: 30%, Communication style: 15%, Educational background: 15%"). Confidence levels can accompany these assessments for different areas, rather than a single aggregate score. Managers can be provided with visual dashboards that highlight candidate strengths and potential growth areas, and "similar candidate" comparisons can be included to help contextualize assessments.

For candidates, feedback reports should focus on actionable insights rather than numerical scores, for example, "If you had held an industry-standard certification in information security, you would have qualified." This also works as constructive growth recommendations rather than simply justifying rejection.

Generally, TalentMatch must restructure its system to enhance rather than replace human judgment. The system should be positioned as a decision support tool rather than an autonomous selection mechanism, and its limitations and positioning should be clearly communicated to hiring managers.

Deployers should review hiring processes, not merely replacing a hiring officer with AI output. Human officers should evaluate qualities the AI cannot effectively assess, such as cultural contribution, creative thinking, and interpersonal dynamics. These can then be used to complement the AI output, thus creating workflows that leverage both AI's data processing capabilities and humans' contextual judgment. Further missing is verification of AI performance. TalentMatch should perform regular audits of algorithm weights, inputs, and baseline fairness metrics. Its customers should conduct ongoing analysis of selection patterns, diversity outcomes, and hiring manager behavior. TalentMatch should consider regular review sessions with diverse stakeholders, and create feedback mechanisms for capturing insights from hiring managers and candidates.

A well-known risk that TalentMatch's system likely encodes is Western cultural assumptions about ideal candidates. This can be prevented through audits for potentially biased evaluation criteria (e.g., prioritizing direct communication styles, individual achievement emphasis, or specific educational institutions), cultural validation testing with diverse stakeholder groups, and the creation of culturally adaptive assessment frameworks that recognize different expressions of professional competence. Training for both the AI system and hiring managers on recognizing cultural bias may be useful.

Chapter 9

Although we don't have any specific examples to suggest here (if we had, we'd include them in the chapter text), here are some guidelines to evaluate your answers (a positive answer in any of these questions implies that you are on to something):

- Does this particular use of AI contradict our collective values in some way?
- Does this AI application break any laws in at least one country?
- Would this kind of process be better off being restricted and mitigated if possible?
- Would this AI hurt more people than it would benefit?
  Would someone want to invest resources in tackling this, e.g., through a company or an NPO?

Index

www.ingramcontent.com/pod-product-compliance
Lightning Source LLC
Chambersburg PA
CBHW080529060326

40690CB00022B/5072